WELCOME TO...

Published by
Princeton Architectural Press
37 East Seventh Street
New York, New York 10003

For a free catalog of books, call 1.800.722.6657.
Visit our web site at www.papress.com.

Printed and bound in Hong Kong
07 06 05 04 5 4 3 2 1 First edition

Editing: Clare Jacobson
Special thanks to: Nettie Aljian, Nicola Bednarek, Janet Behning, Megan Carey, Penny (Yuen Pik) Chu, Russell Fernandez, Jan Haux, Mark Lamster, Nancy Eklund Later, Linda Lee, Nancy Levinson, Katharine Myers, Jane Sheinman, Scott Tennent, Jennifer Thompson, Joe Weston, and Deb Wood of Princeton Architectural Press —Kevin C. Lippert, publisher

Library of Congress Cataloging-in-Publication Data
Empire / edited by Nicholas Oscar Blechman.
p. cm. — (Nozone ; 9)
ISBN 1-56898-457-X (alk. paper)
1. United States—Foreign relations—2001- —Miscellanea. 2. United States—Foreign relations—2001- —Pictorial works. 3. Imperialism—Miscellanea. 4. Imperialism—Pictorial works. 5. Globalization—Miscellanea. 6. Globalization—Pictorial works. 7. Civilization, Modern—American influences—Miscellanea. 8. Civilization, Modern—American influences—Pictorial works. 9. Protest literature, American. 10. Politics in art—United States. I. Blechman, Nicholas. II. Series.
PN6700.N69 vol. 9
[E895]
325'.32'0973090511—dc22

2003019156

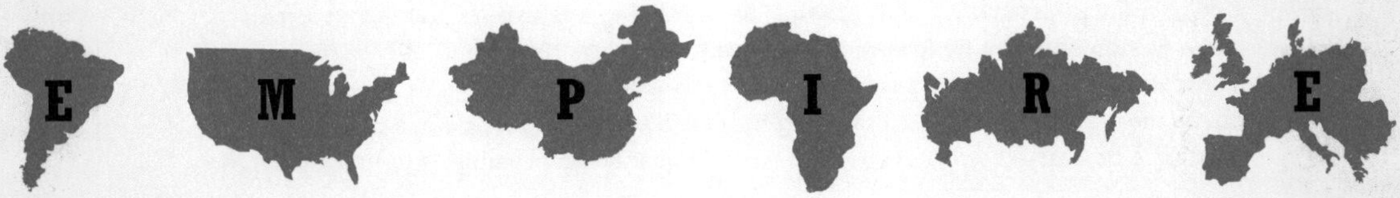

NOZONE IX

Edited by Nicholas Blechman

Princeton Architectural Press, New York

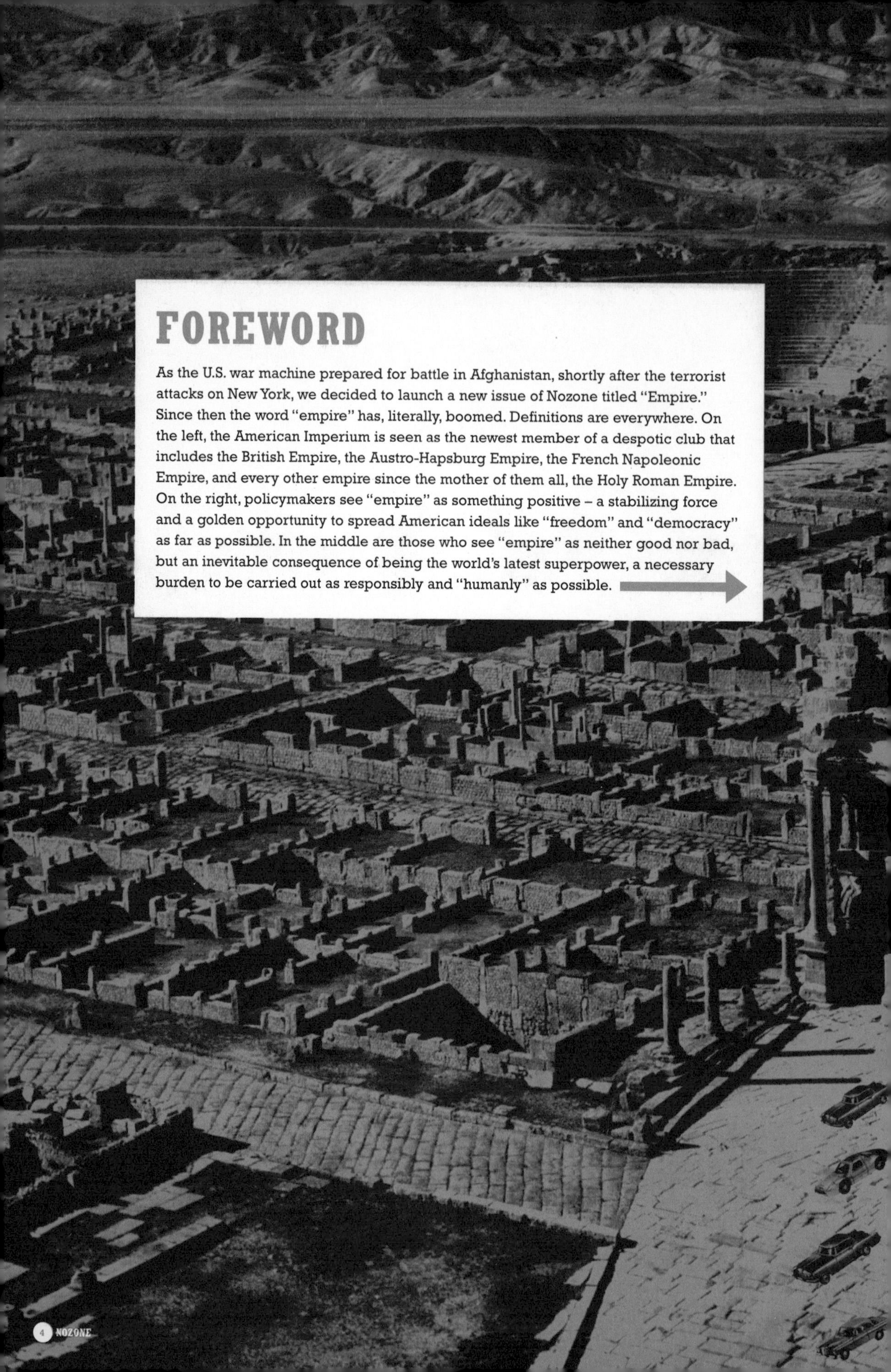

FOREWORD

As the U.S. war machine prepared for battle in Afghanistan, shortly after the terrorist attacks on New York, we decided to launch a new issue of Nozone titled "Empire." Since then the word "empire" has, literally, boomed. Definitions are everywhere. On the left, the American Imperium is seen as the newest member of a despotic club that includes the British Empire, the Austro-Hapsburg Empire, the French Napoleonic Empire, and every other empire since the mother of them all, the Holy Roman Empire. On the right, policymakers see "empire" as something positive – a stabilizing force and a golden opportunity to spread American ideals like "freedom" and "democracy" as far as possible. In the middle are those who see "empire" as neither good nor bad, but an inevitable consequence of being the world's latest superpower, a necessary burden to be carried out as responsibly and "humanly" as possible.

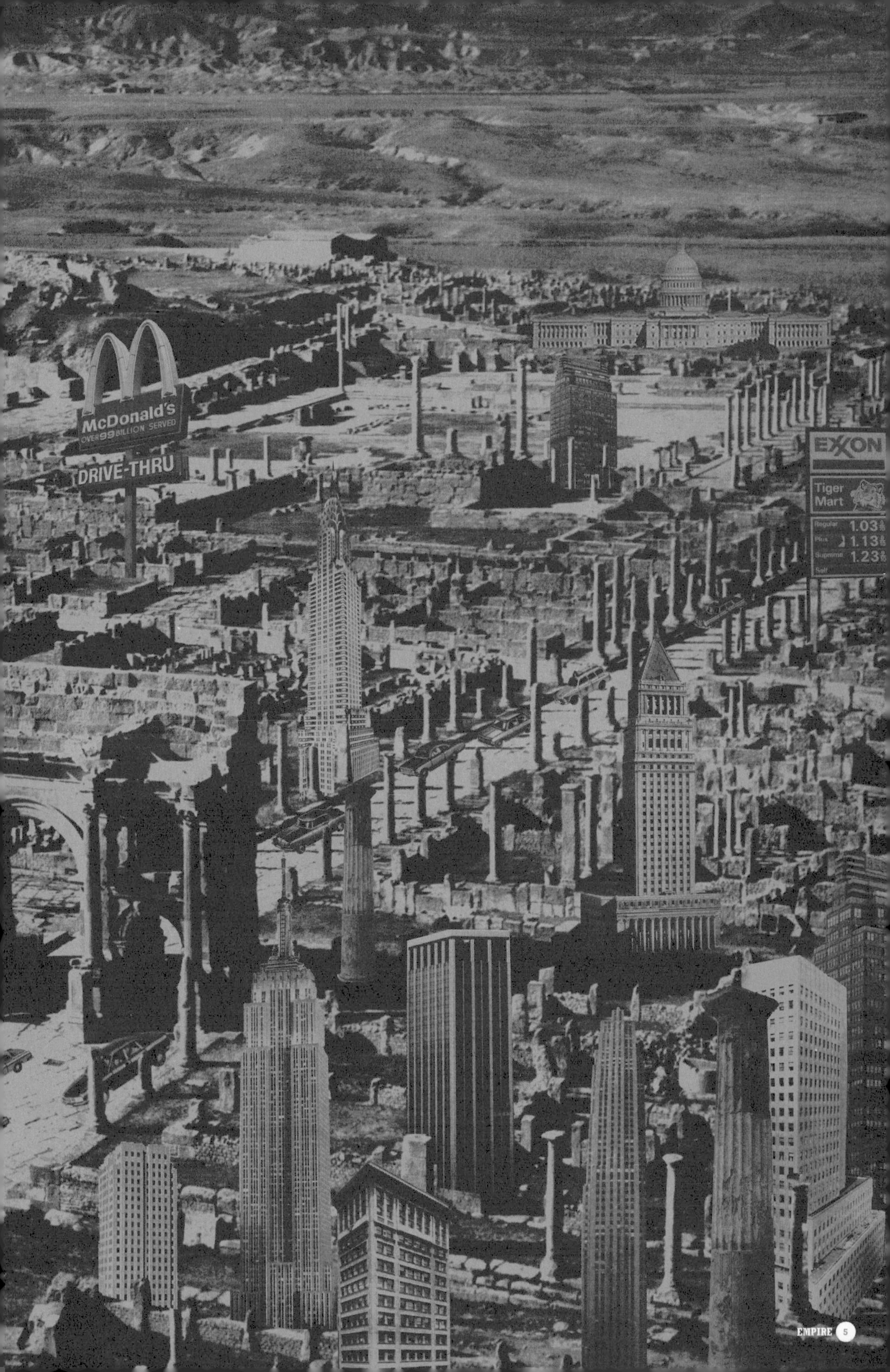

McDonald's
OVER 99 BILLION SERVED
DRIVE-THRU
EXXON
Tiger Mart
Regular 1.03
Plus 1.13
Supreme 1.23

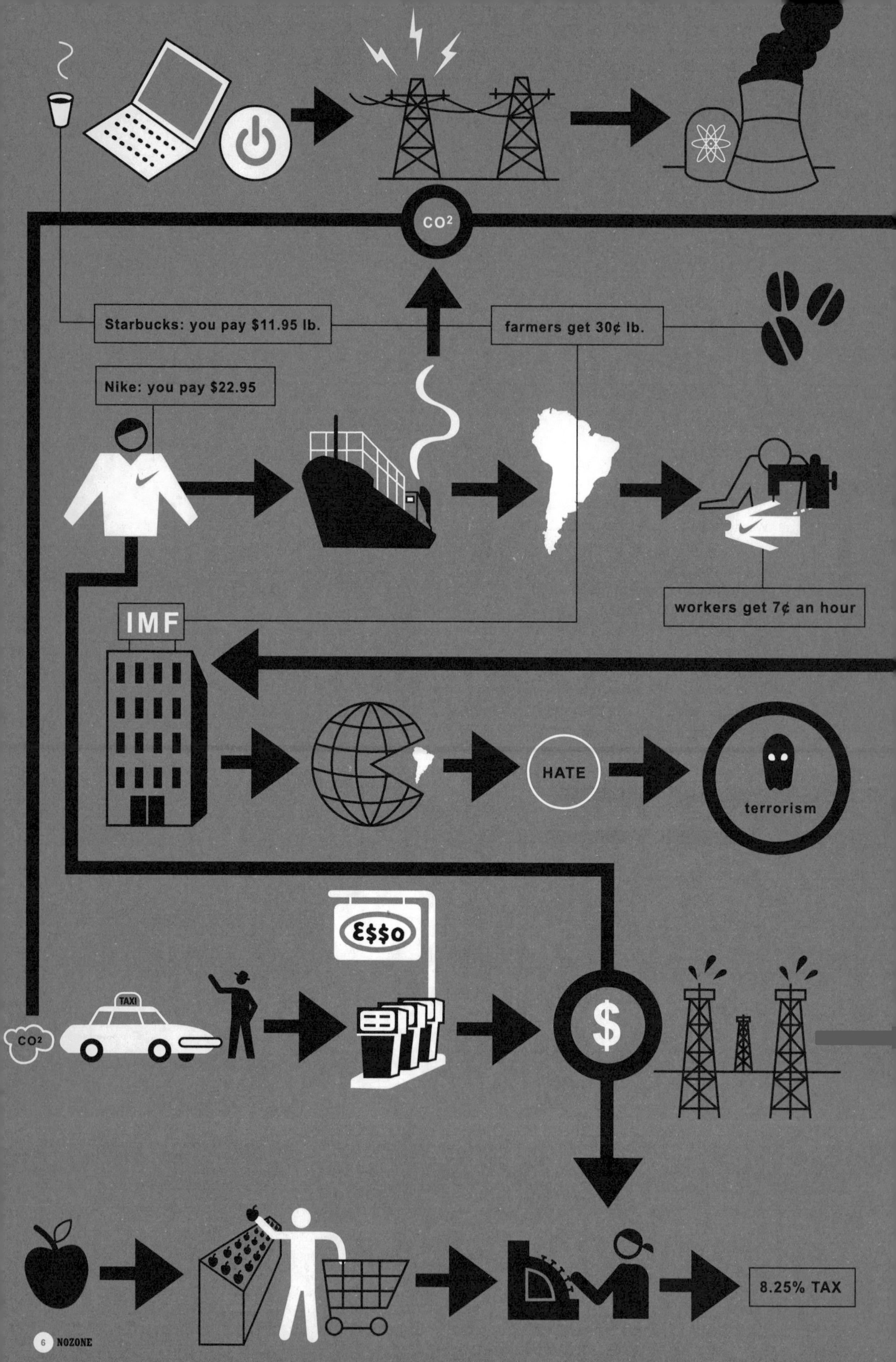
CO2
Starbucks: you pay $11.95 lb.
farmers get 30¢ lb.
Nike: you pay $22.95
workers get 7¢ an hour
IMF
HATE
terrorism
E$$O
TAXI
CO2
$
8.25% TAX

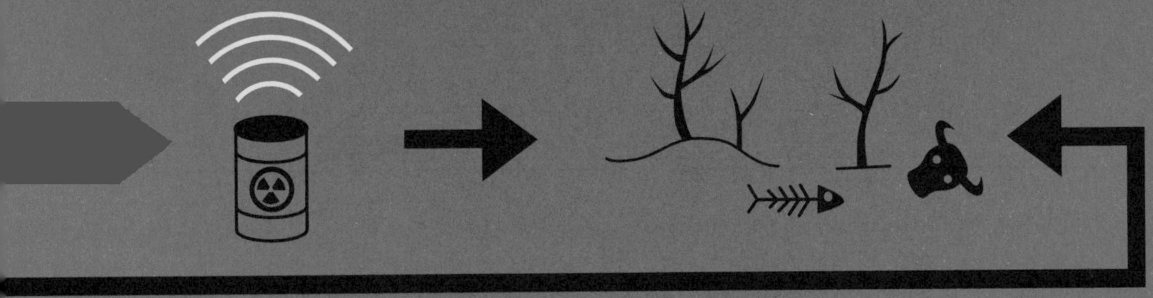

For us, "empire" refers to something different. In fact it doesn't refer to any one thing, but to a vast matrix of forces and counterforces. Billions drink its sodas, listen to its music, breathe its air, drive its cars, smoke its tobacco, practice its religions, watch its movies, ingest its pharmaceuticals, pay its debts, and benefit or suffer from its policies. From the life-altering patterns of our DNA to the chemical workings of our brains, from the melting ice caps in Antarctica to the defoliated wastelands of Africa, its relentless expansion goes unchecked.

Pinpointing the heart of such an empire is impossible. Though there are some obvious suspects (the IMF, the World Bank, the U.S.A.), its nature as a network constantly defies accurate denunciation. Instead, its power lies in its very connectivity. Data, capital, cargo, media, and marketing flow around us with dizzying speed and dexterity. We have no idea, for example, that by wearing a certain sweatshirt we are contributing to labor abuse in North Korea (see page 62); that by using an ATM in Beirut, we are making a donation to the fortune of a banker in Boston (see page 66); or that by starting our car we are tacitly endorsing a war in the oil fields of the Middle East (see CNN!). These connections exist, but, hidden in the voluptuous vastness of the empire, they become invisible.

And its effects cut deeper still because empire has, in its often illusive way, imbedded itself beneath our skins. It has become an aesthetic, a conditioning, a psychology, a lifestyle. For us a movie being shown simultaneously in hundreds of theaters across the country, across the continent, and across the globe, is nothing new. We take for granted the Nike logo on our sock, the Starbucks logo on our coffee cup, the cell

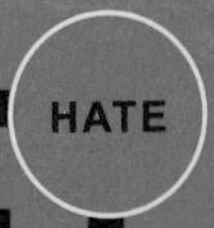

phone in our hand, and the war in Iraq viewed from the comfort of our living rooms. And not only are we unsurprised by these things, we quite often demand them. So where does our individuality end, and the empire begin? And to what extent, no matter who we think we are, are we all imperialists?

Whatever the answers to these questions may be, one thing seems certain: the "imperial mood" is growing darker by the day. But as the lotus rises from the mud, so the seeds of revolution sprout from the depths of our multinational smog. Antiwar demonstrations and other protests shake the globe with a fury, a volume, and a sophistication never before seen. From inside corporations themselves, there are signs of rebellion (see page 152) while nation-states struggle to control populations that are actively inventing entirely new forms of governance by employing the very technologies used to oppress them.

In this spirit, Nozone rallies a coalition of artists, designers, photographers, and writers to protest what appears to be the monolithic state of our civilization on the cusp of the twenty-first century. Welcome to Nozone IX.

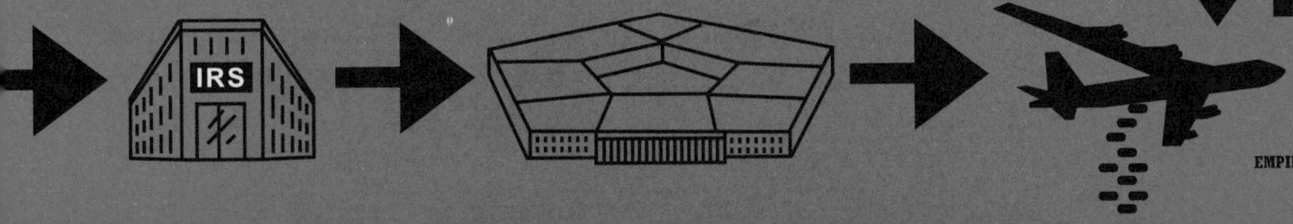

CONTENTS

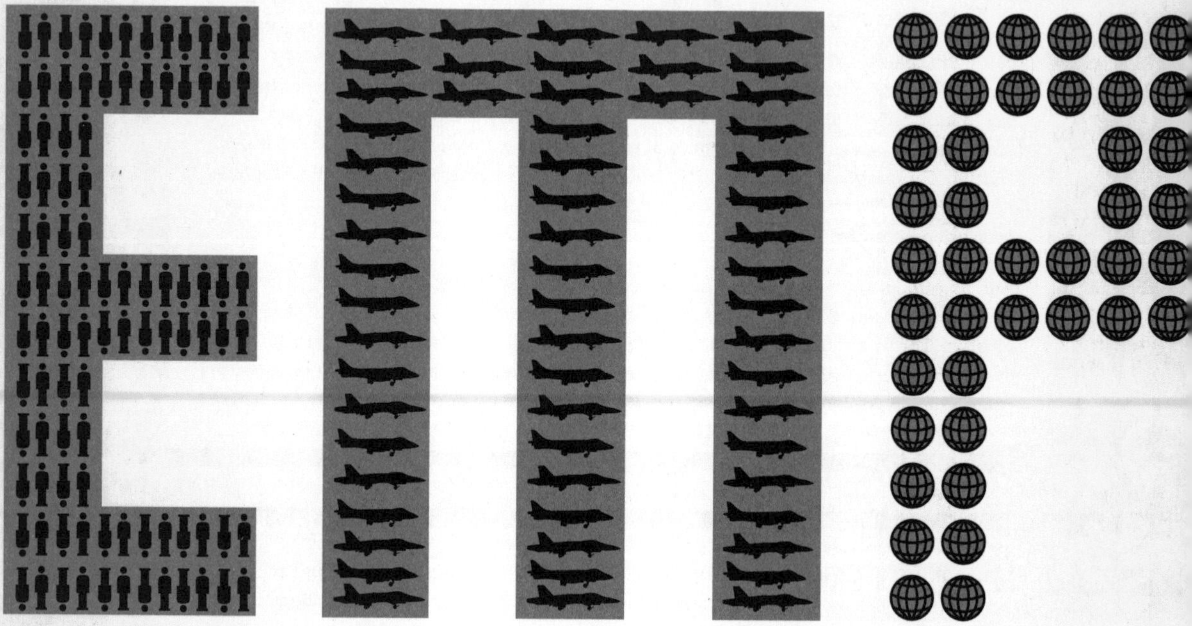

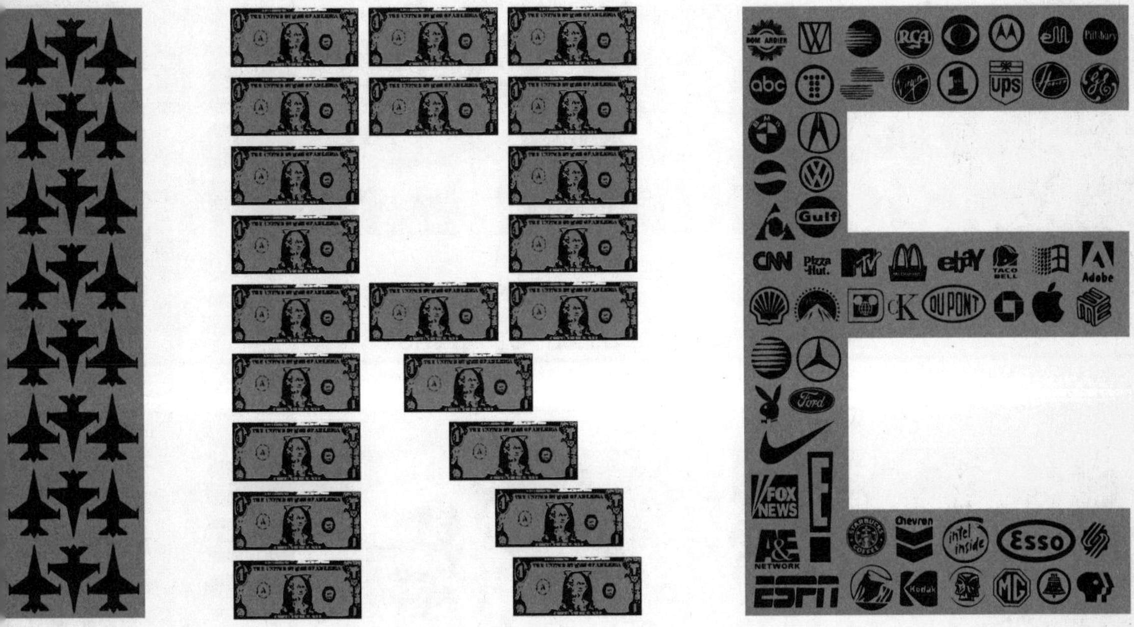

EDITOR: Nicholas Blechman
EDITORIAL COLLABORATOR: Jesse Gordon
DESIGN: Knickerbocker Design

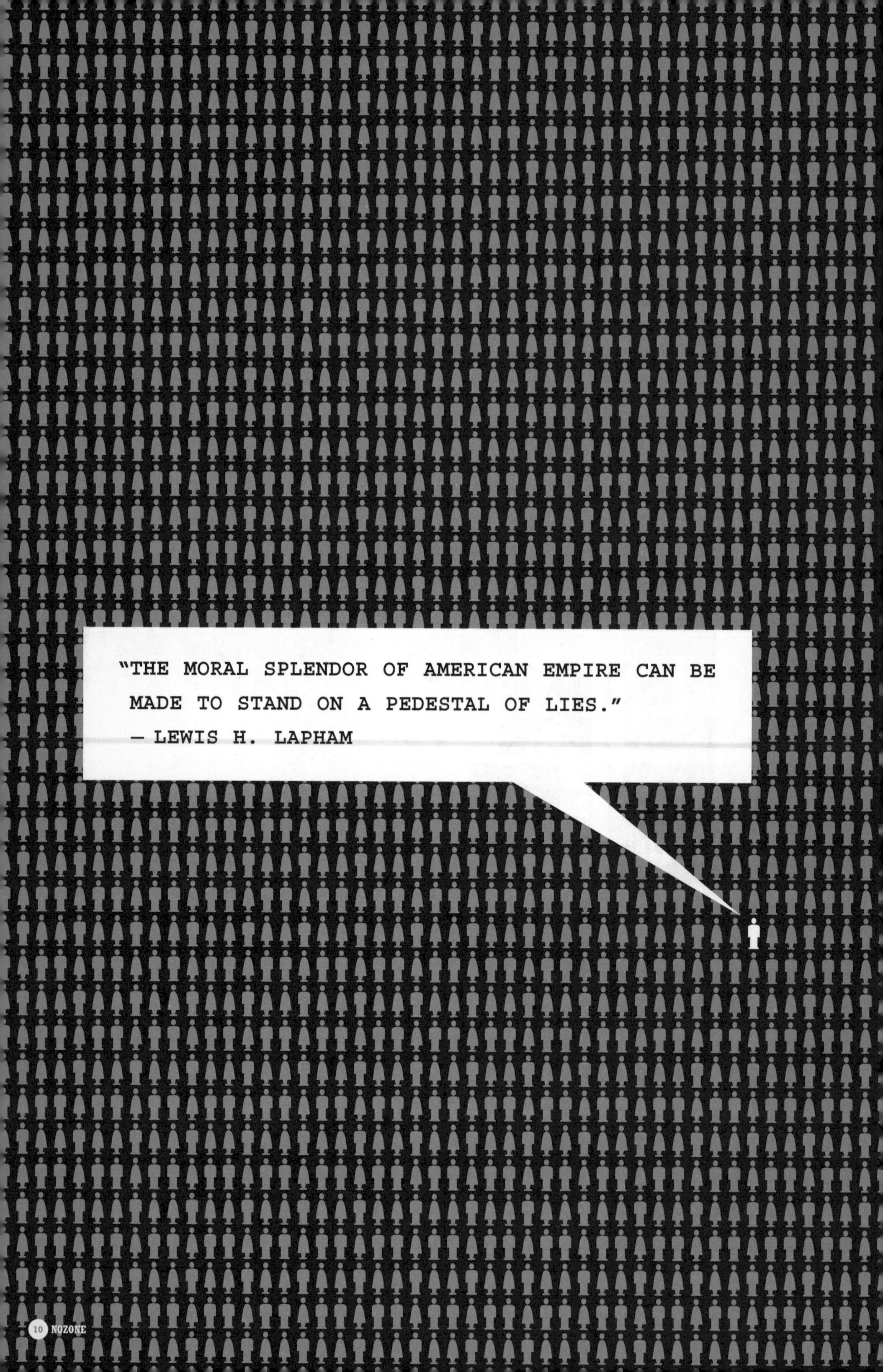
"THE MORAL SPLENDOR OF AMERICAN EMPIRE CAN BE MADE TO STAND ON A PEDESTAL OF LIES."
— LEWIS H. LAPHAM

Ceci n'est pas une comic
This is not...
a pipe.
This is not...
an invasion.
This is not...
pollution.
This is not...
UNEMPLOYMENT
unemployment.
This is not...
necessary.
This is not...
dangerous.
This is not...
your concern.
This is not...
a problem.
So...
do I have your vote?
with apologies to Magritte
Peter Kuper

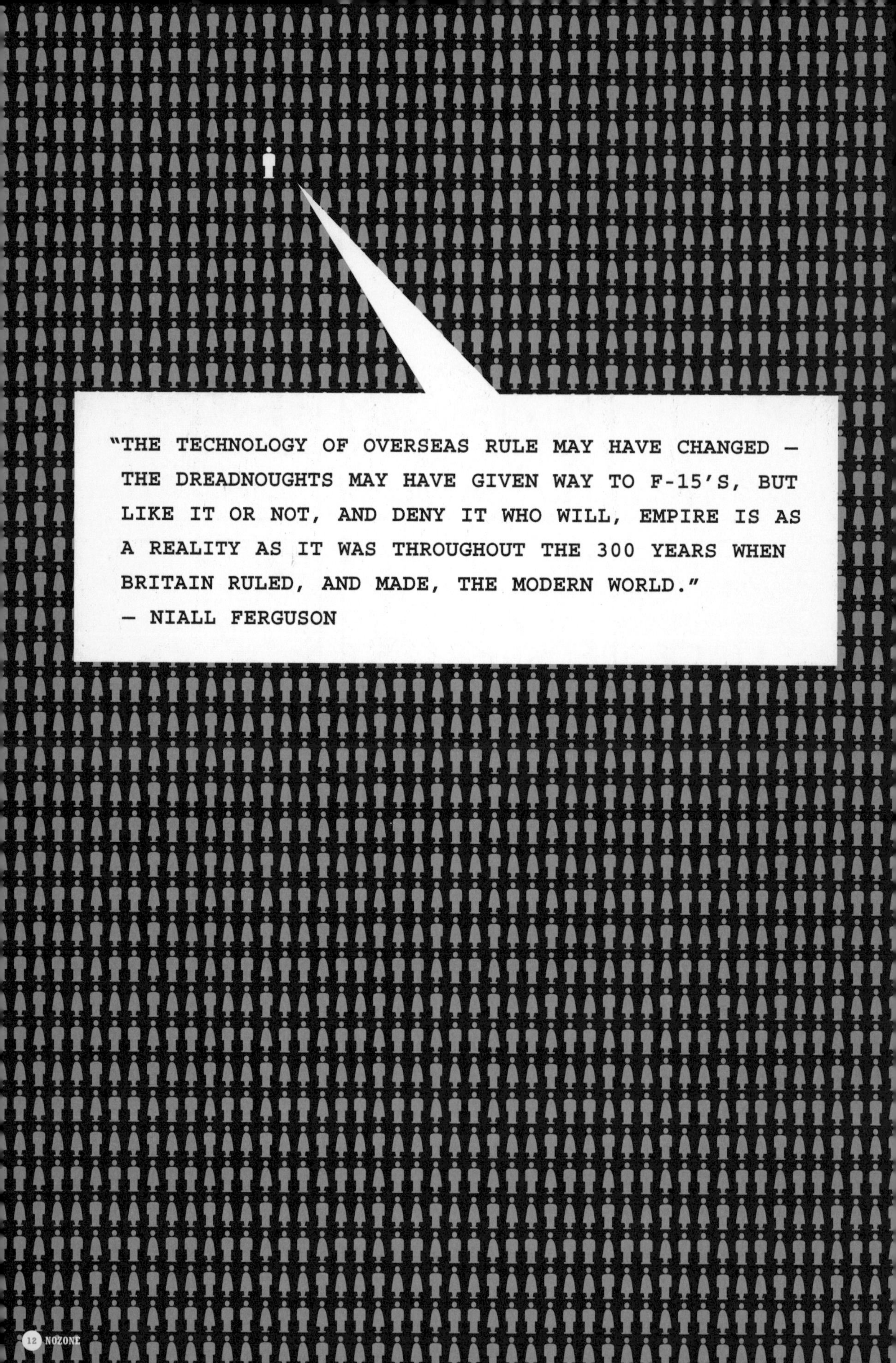
"THE TECHNOLOGY OF OVERSEAS RULE MAY HAVE CHANGED – THE DREADNOUGHTS MAY HAVE GIVEN WAY TO F-15'S, BUT LIKE IT OR NOT, AND DENY IT WHO WILL, EMPIRE IS AS A REALITY AS IT WAS THROUGHOUT THE 300 YEARS WHEN BRITAIN RULED, AND MADE, THE MODERN WORLD."
– NIALL FERGUSON

AM I AN IMPERIALIST?

				ANSWER
Which of the following symbols are you most conscious of on a daily basis?	 1	 2	 3	
Which of the following skills do you think is most valuable to master in the modern world?	 1	 3	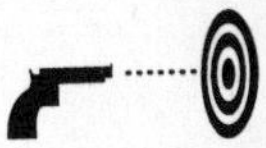 2	
Which of the following insignias do you most frequently see displayed in public?	 1	 2	 3	
Which of the following images do you most associate with the general character of your countrymen?	 3	 1	 2	
Which of the following best represents the driving force behind most of your countrymen's behavior?	 2	 1	 3	
Which of the following words do you most frequently hear your politicians use?	POLLUTION 1	WAR 2	GOD 3	
Add up the small numbers next to each of your answers. If you score lower than 8 then congratulations you do not live in an empire. If you score between 6 and 10 then you may live in an empire but might not be fully conscious of it. If you score above 10 then you definitely live in an empire, are definitely conscious of it, and should do something about it.				TOTAL

I AM NOT AN

IMPERIALIST

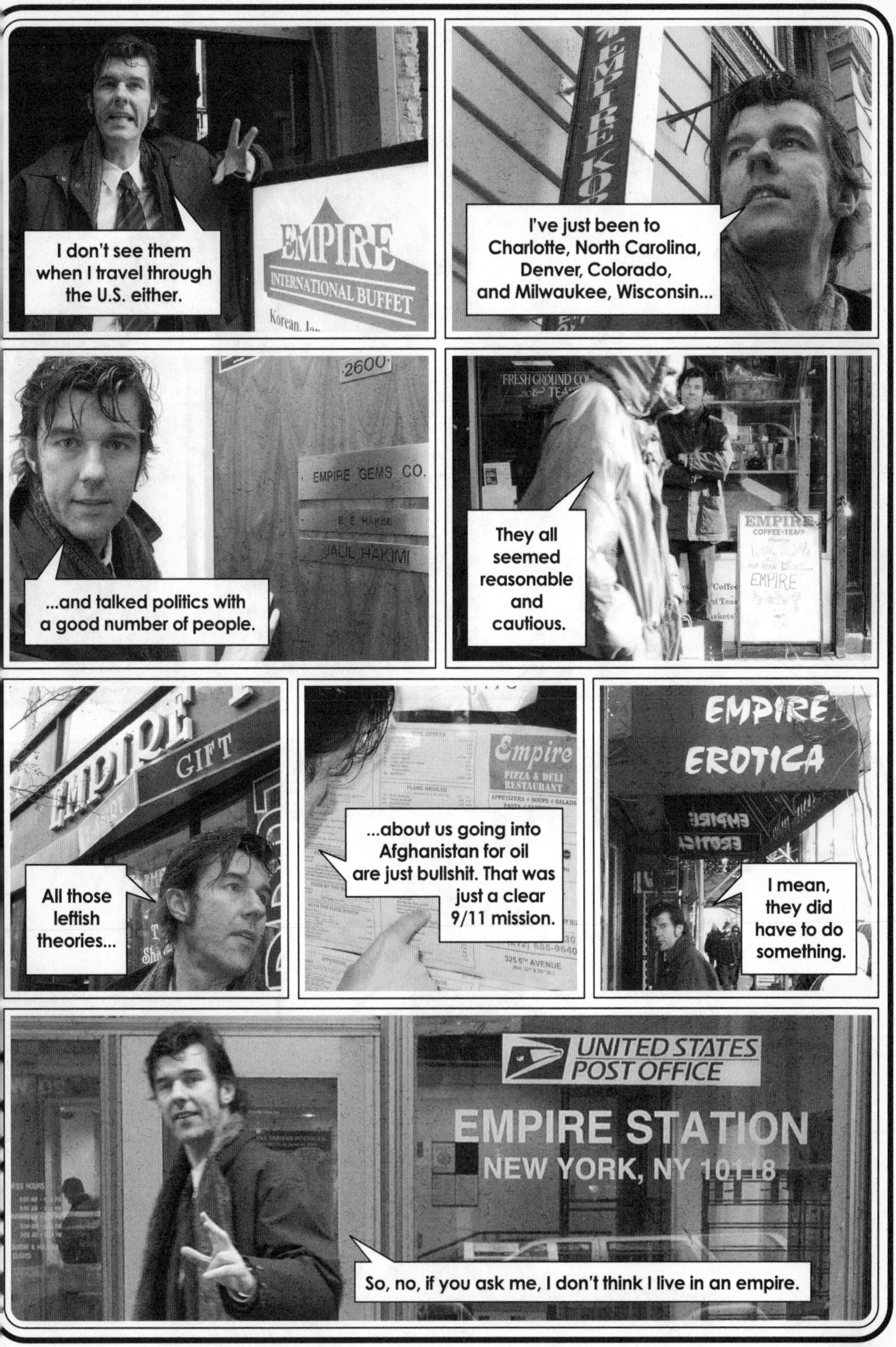
EMPIRE
INTERNATIONAL BUFFET
I don't see them when I travel through the U.S. either.
EMPIRE
I've just been to Charlotte, North Carolina, Denver, Colorado, and Milwaukee, Wisconsin...
2600
EMPIRE GEMS CO.
JALIL HAKIMI
...and talked politics with a good number of people.
EMPIRE
COFFEE & TEAS
They all seemed reasonable and cautious.
EMPIRE
GIFT
All those leftish theories...
Empire
PIZZA & DELI RESTAURANT
...about us going into Afghanistan for oil are just bullshit. That was just a clear 9/11 mission.
EMPIRE
EROTICA
I mean, they did have to do something.
UNITED STATES POST OFFICE
EMPIRE STATION
NEW YORK, NY 10118
So, no, if you ask me, I don't think I live in an empire.

FIN

Lukova
war is not the answer

OF HYMN POWER

HAVING TRIUMPHED IN THE MILLENNIAL WARS, WE RETIRED TO OUR HOME ON HIGH—THE FLOATING CLOUDS OF JOY—WHERE WE LIVED IN A STATE OF RAPTURE, SECURE UNDER THE REIGN OF OUR GLORIOUS DYNASTY.

FAR BELOW, PAGAN SAVAGES AND MUTANT APOSTATES SCAVENGED THE RAVAGED PLANET TO PAY TRIBUTE TO OUR CELESTIAL FLOATING REPUBLIC.

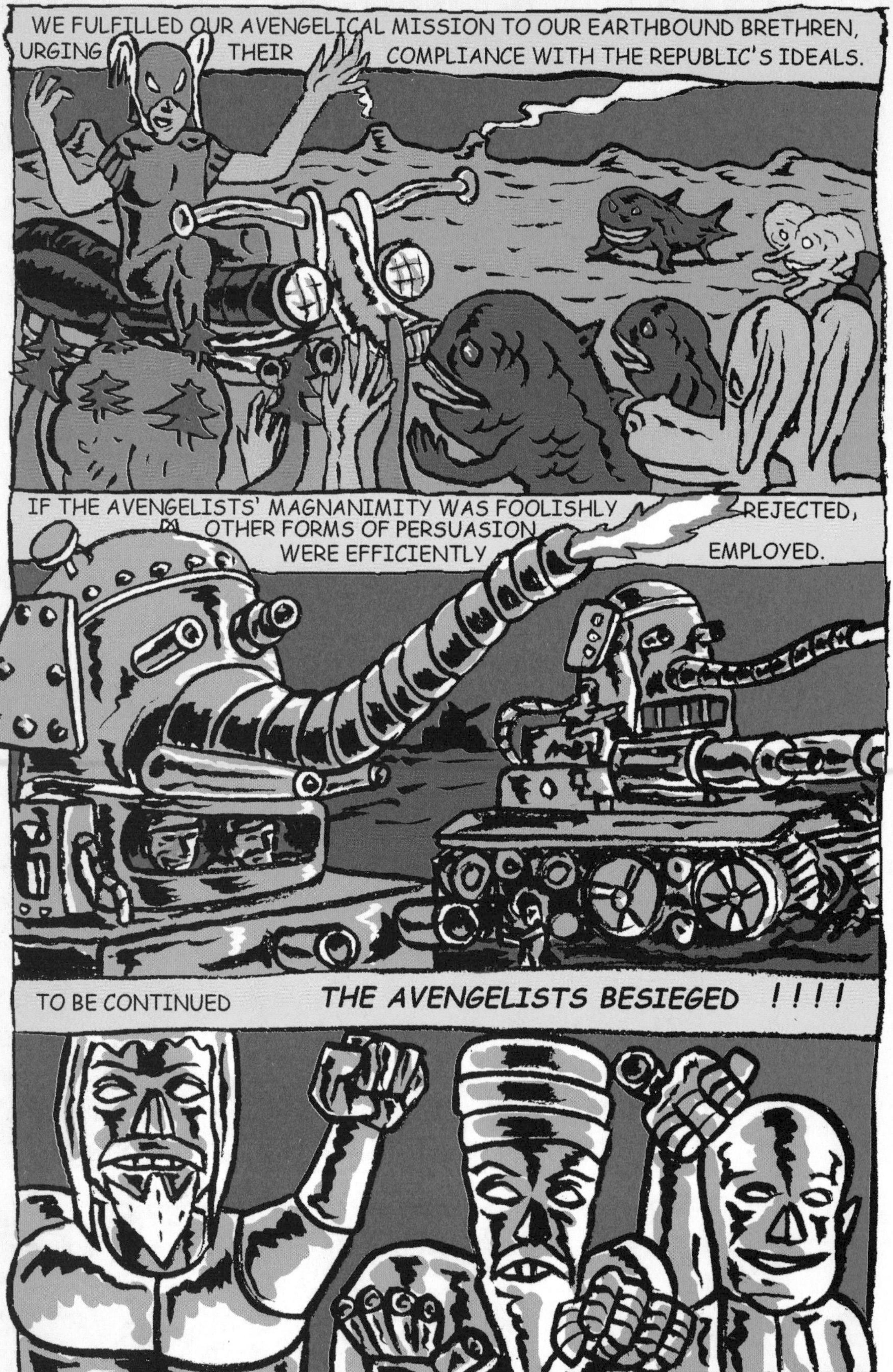
WE FULFILLED OUR AVENGELICAL MISSION TO OUR EARTHBOUND BRETHREN, URGING THEIR COMPLIANCE WITH THE REPUBLIC'S IDEALS.
IF THE AVENGELISTS' MAGNANIMITY WAS FOOLISHLY REJECTED, OTHER FORMS OF PERSUASION WERE EFFICIENTLY EMPLOYED.
TO BE CONTINUED
THE AVENGELISTS BESIEGED !!!!

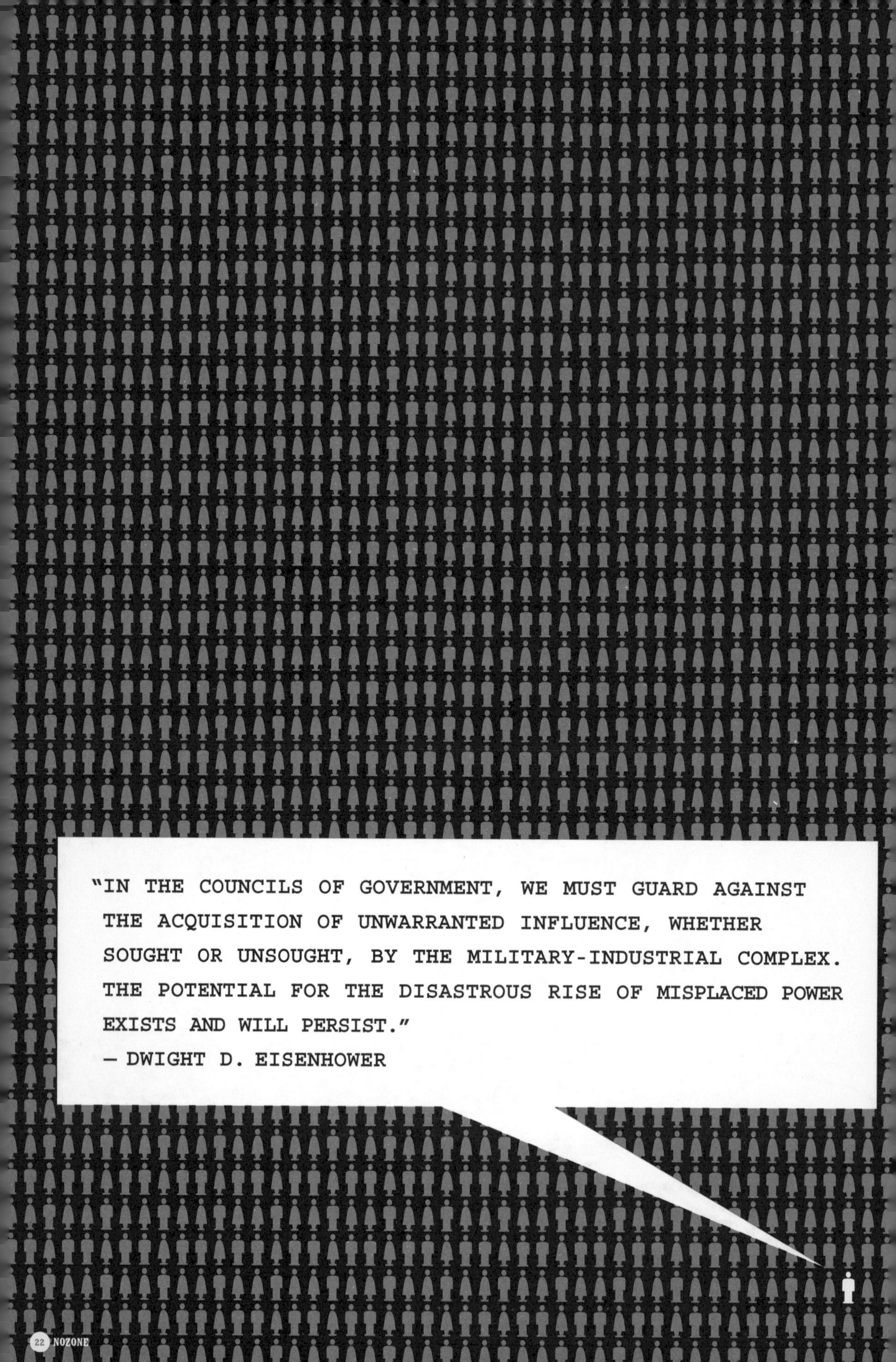
"IN THE COUNCILS OF GOVERNMENT, WE MUST GUARD AGAINST THE ACQUISITION OF UNWARRANTED INFLUENCE, WHETHER SOUGHT OR UNSOUGHT, BY THE MILITARY-INDUSTRIAL COMPLEX. THE POTENTIAL FOR THE DISASTROUS RISE OF MISPLACED POWER EXISTS AND WILL PERSIST."
— DWIGHT D. EISENHOWER

EMPIRICAL OBSERVATIONS
THROUGHOUT THE COURSE OF HISTORY EMPIRES HAVE ALL SHARED ONE COMMON BELIEF...
SIZE MATTERS.
N
AS A RULE, EMPIRES TEND TO INVOKE A HIGHER AUTHORITY.
YOU MAY RAPE, PILLAGE, LOOT, MURDER, PLUNDER, ETC., BUT ONLY IN THE NAME OF GOD.
EMPIRES POSSESS THE PECULIAR ABILITY TO SIMULTANEOUSLY BE BENEVOLENT AND DESTRUCTIVE.
YOU'RE LIBERATED!
THEY HAVE ALSO BEEN KNOWN TO MAKE SIGNIFICANT CONTRIBUTIONS.
BEHOLD THE OTTOMAN!
AND WHILE EMPIRES LIKE TO THINK THEY'LL LAST FOREVER...
2000 YEARS HENCE PEOPLE WILL STILL ATTEND TOGA PARTIES.
DELPHI
...THEY NEVER DO.
IF YOU LOOK DOWN TO YOUR LEFT, YOU GET A SPLENDID VIEW OF ANCIENT WASHINGTON.
ASTROTOUR 3000
G. Clement

EMPIRICAL DATA

America consumes 52 million gallons of soft drinks per year

The number of cars is increasing 3 times faster than the population

52

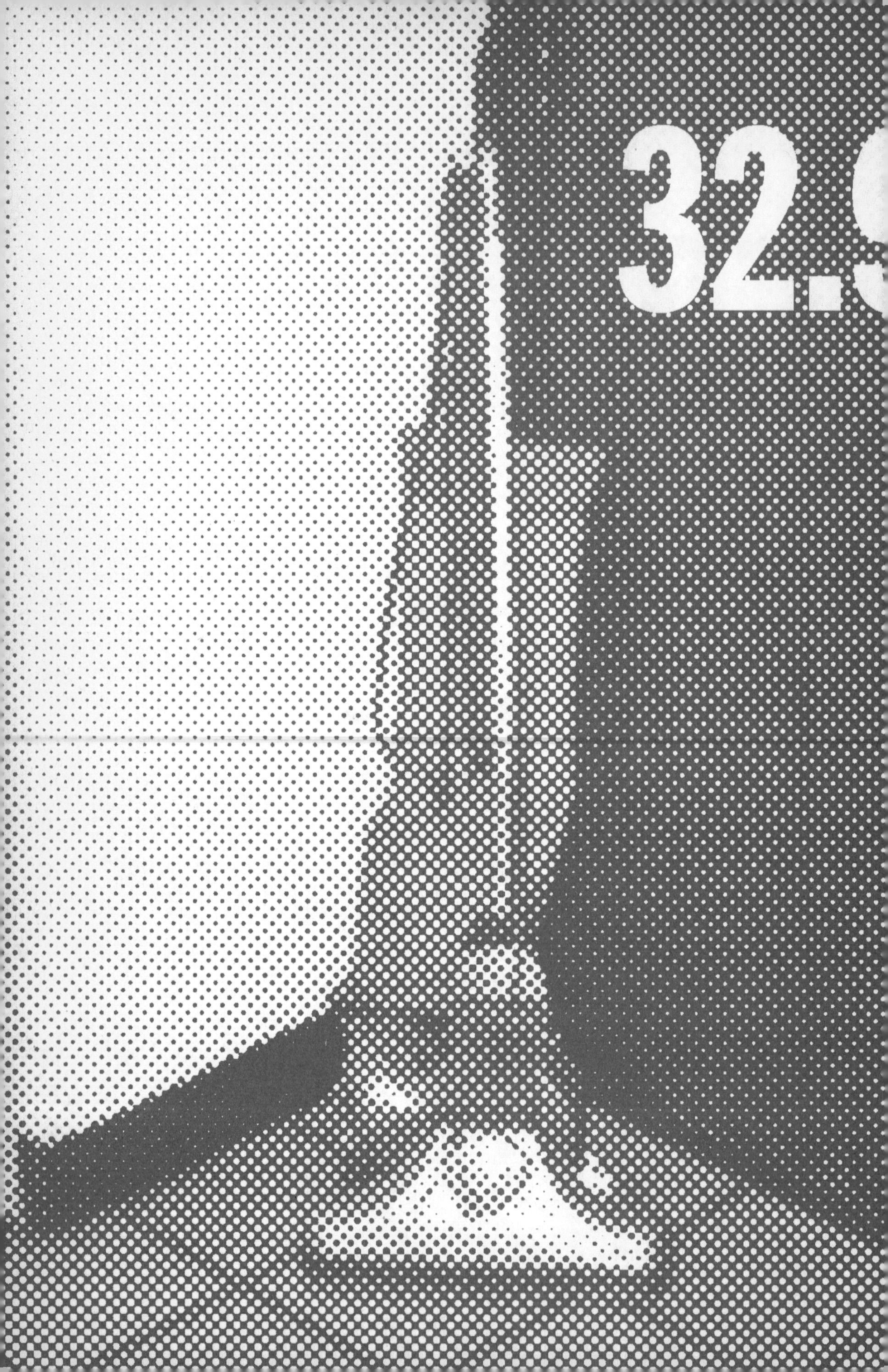
32.

32.9 million Americans live at or below the poverty line.

There are 2 credit cards for every person in the United States.

43% of Americans feel that abortion is legalized murder.

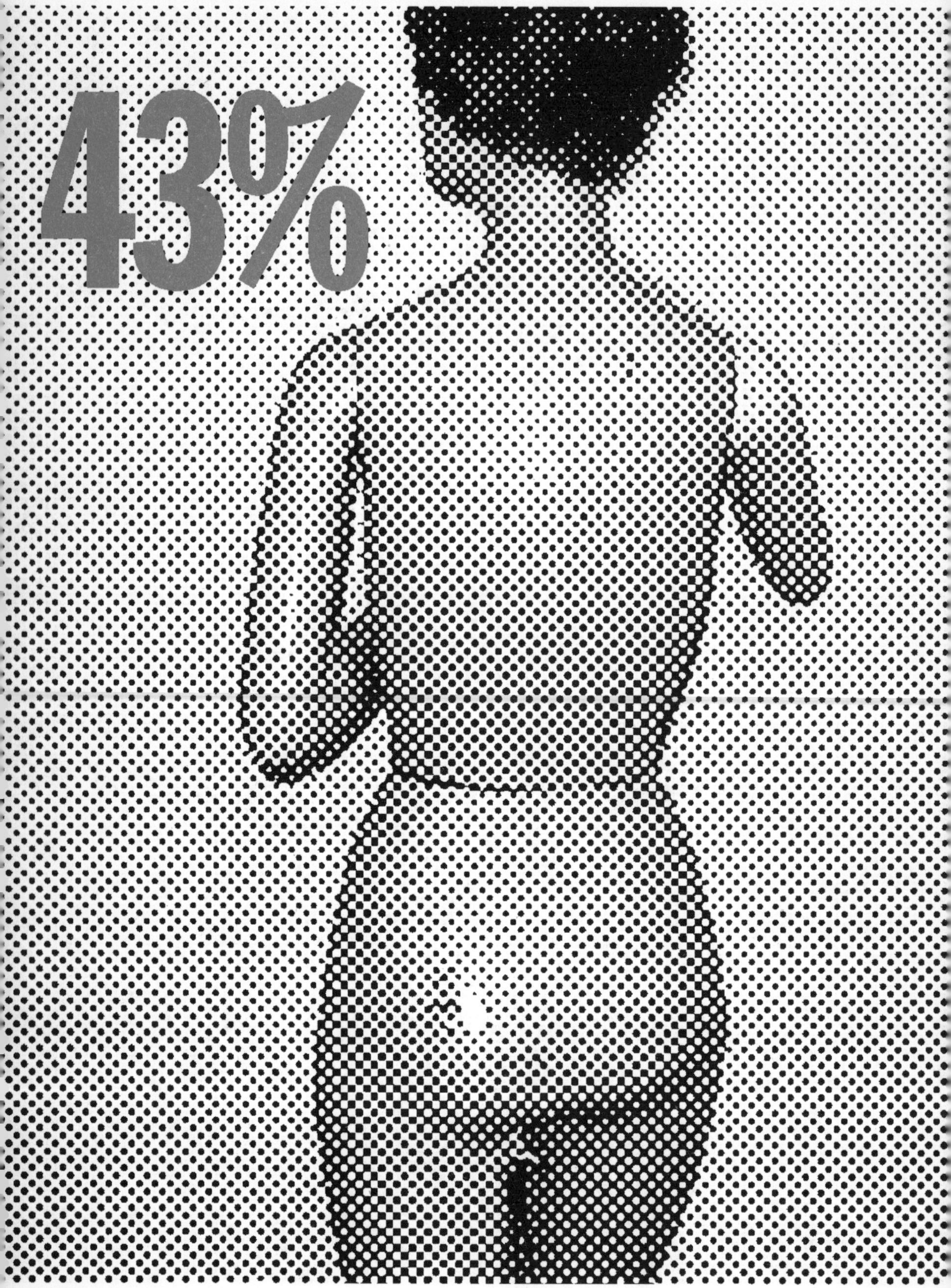

57% of Americans feel that capital punishment is legalized murder.
47% feel that we should stop killing dolphins and whales.

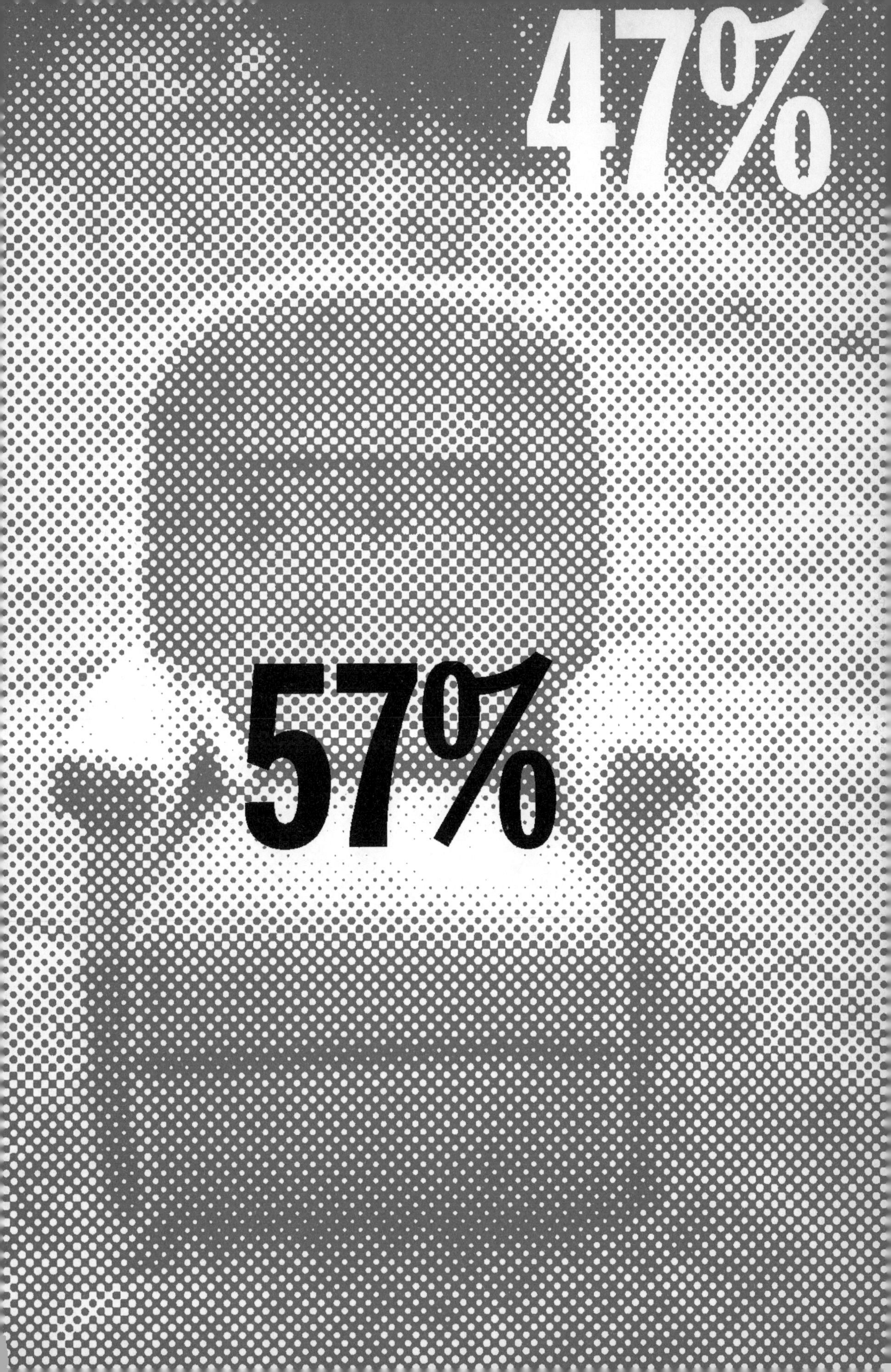
47%
57%

76%82%68%

When Americans were asked to identify by what criteria success should be measured, 76% answered "fame," 32% answered "wealth," and 68% answered "happiness."

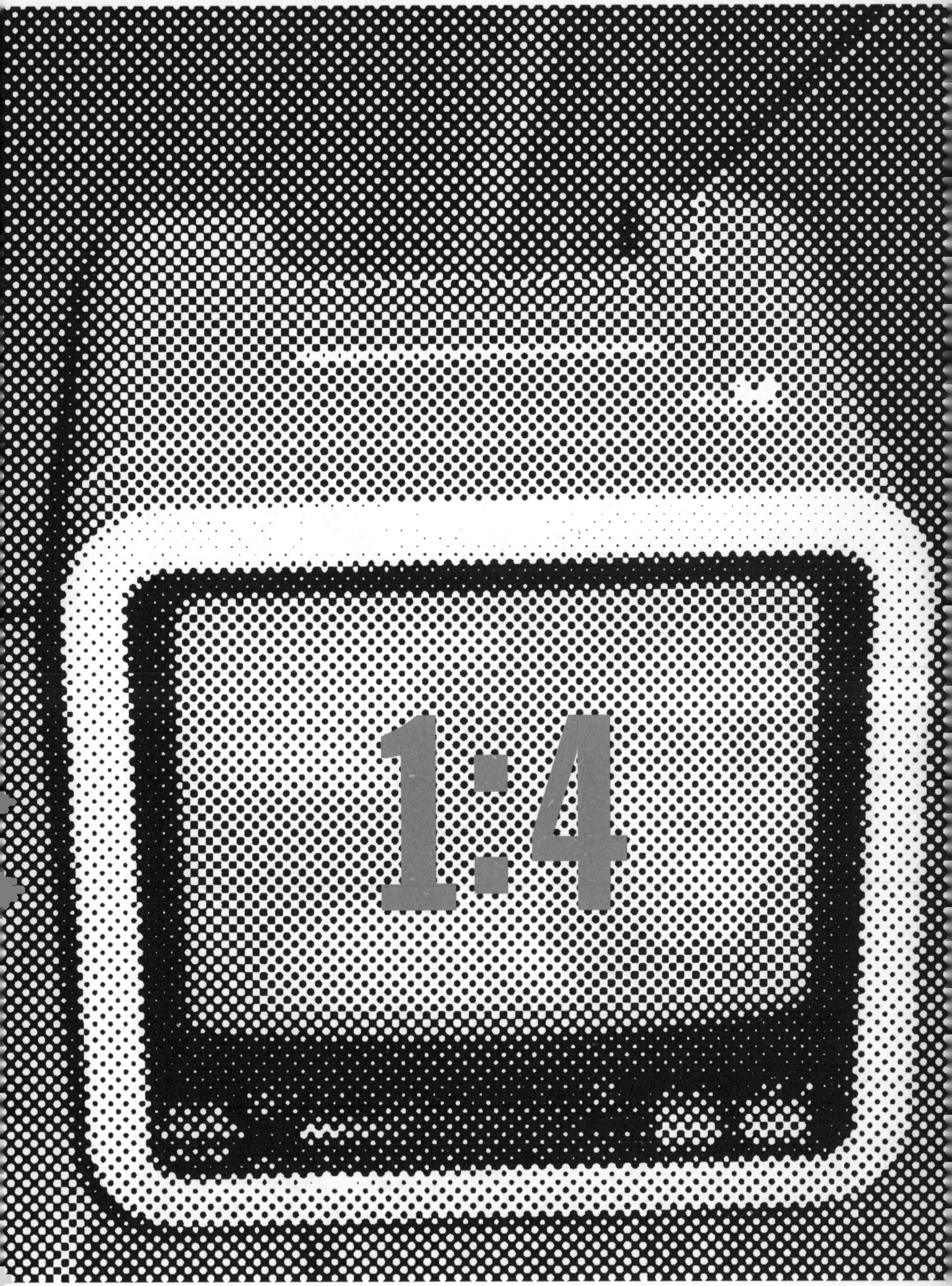

1 in every 4 Americans will appear on television.

47% feel that gun ownership is an American right. 50% feel that responsible gun ownership reduces crime.

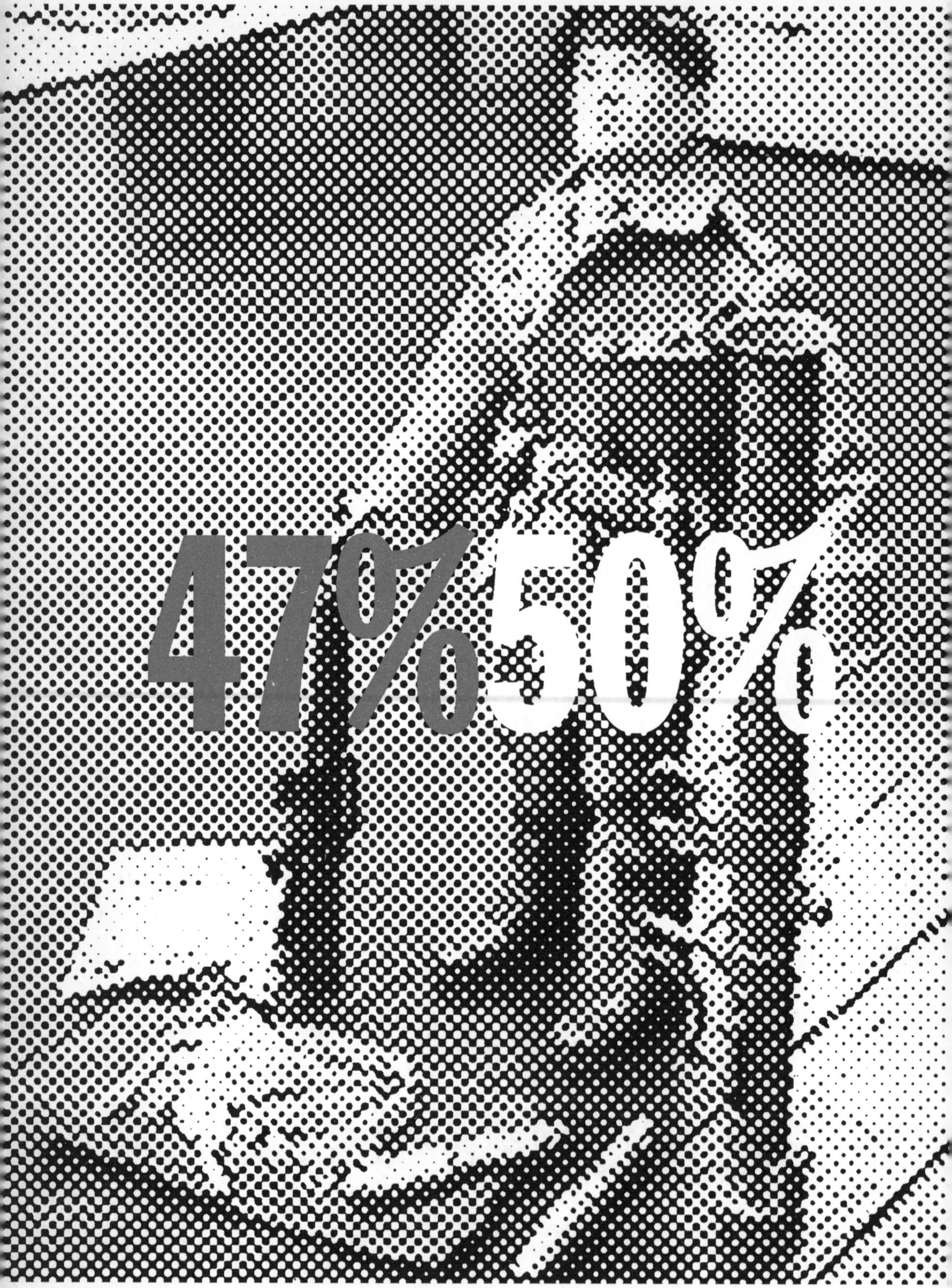

Out of 34,000 gun deaths annually, fewer than 300 are classified "justifiable homicide."

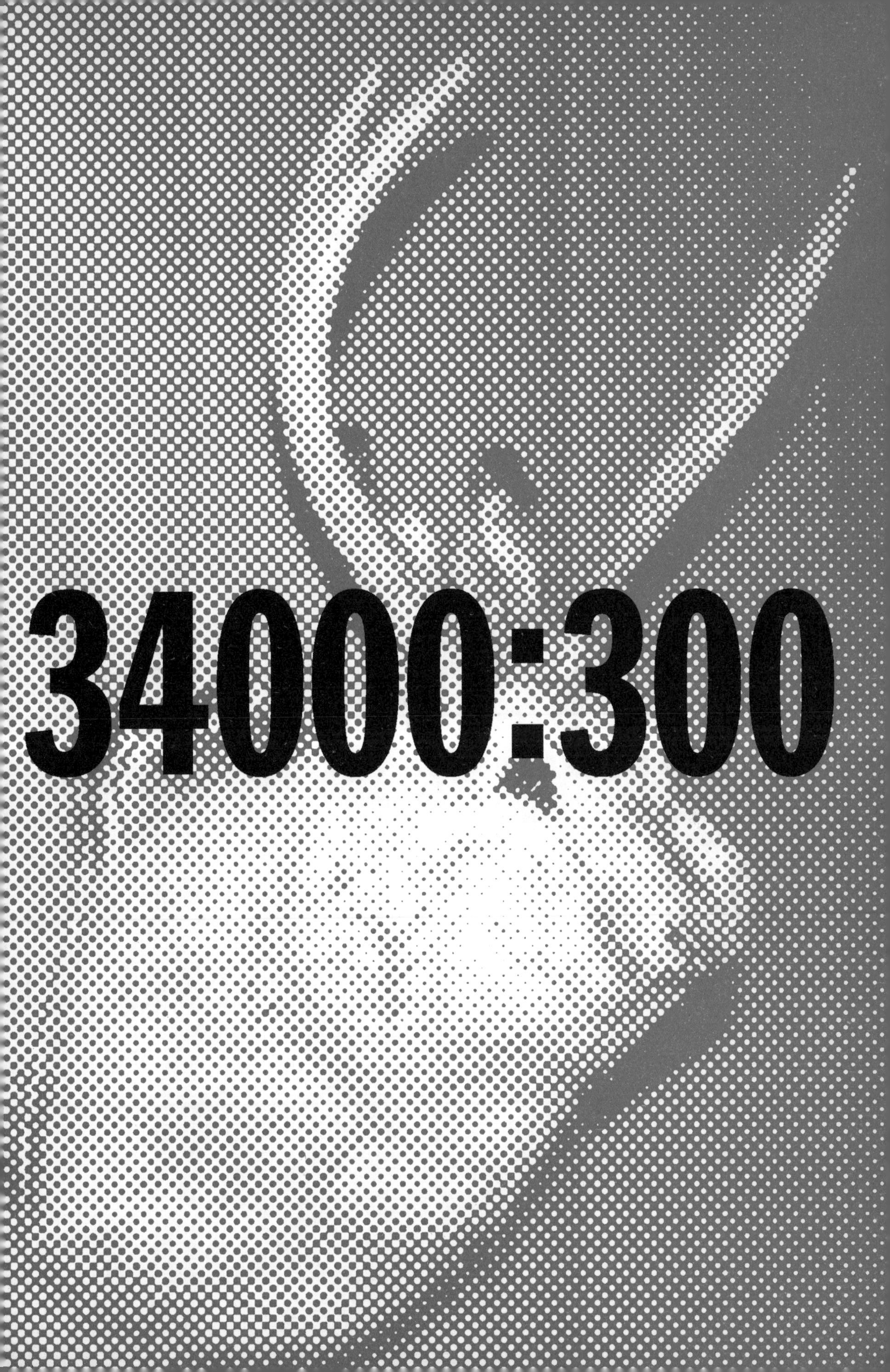
34000:300

57%

% feel that "power" is the greatest of all virtues. 57% feel that "compassion" is the greatest of all virtues.

81% feel that exercising "power" will yield greater rewards than exercising "compassion."

78% feel that American culture, not government, is responsible for our society's ills.

87% feel that America is an "overly litigious" societ

Please note that all facts and figures are meant for entertainment purposes only. They were collected fro numerous websites of varying reputations and are not meant to be taken literall

87%

MK MABRY

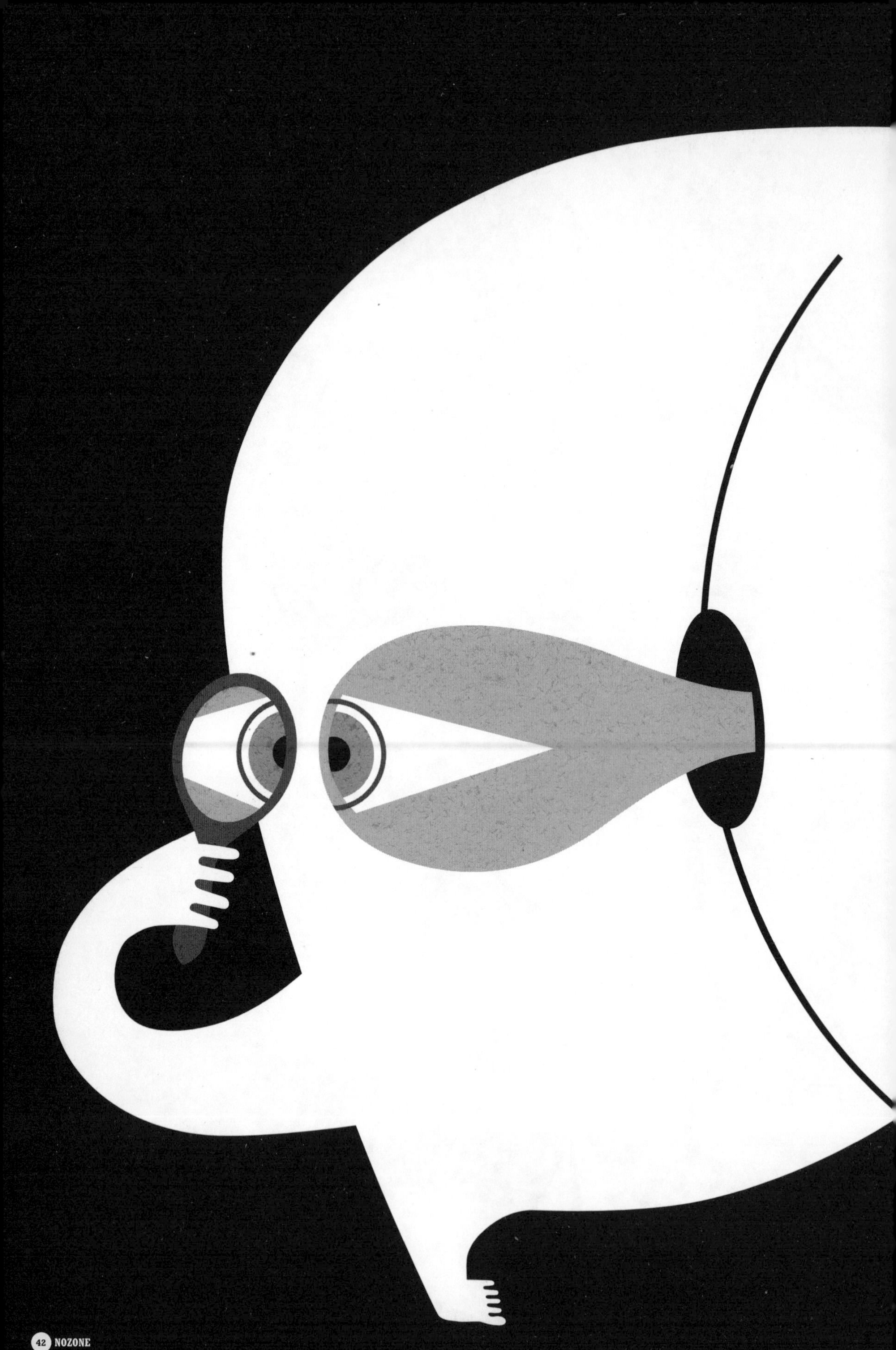

MK MABRY

You should be suspicious when you see a straight line on a map.

— Peter Barber

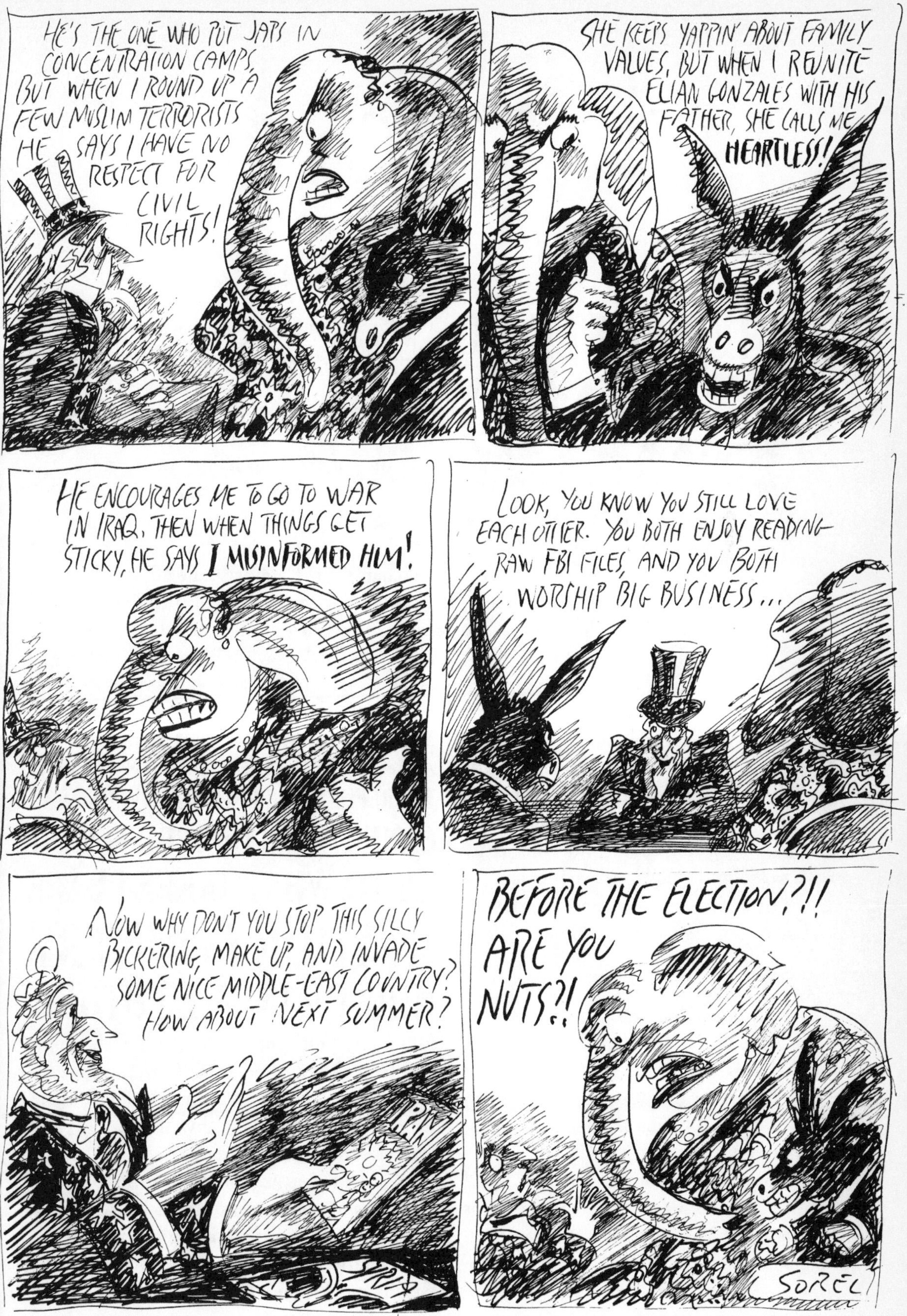
HE'S THE ONE WHO PUT JAPS IN CONCENTRATION CAMPS, BUT WHEN I ROUND UP A FEW MUSLIM TERRORISTS HE SAYS I HAVE NO RESPECT FOR CIVIL RIGHTS!
SHE KEEPS YAPPIN' ABOUT FAMILY VALUES, BUT WHEN I REUNITE ELIAN GONZALES WITH HIS FATHER, SHE CALLS ME HEARTLESS!
HE ENCOURAGES ME TO GO TO WAR IN IRAQ, THEN WHEN THINGS GET STICKY, HE SAYS I MISINFORMED HIM!
LOOK, YOU KNOW YOU STILL LOVE EACH OTHER. YOU BOTH ENJOY READING RAW FBI FILES, AND YOU BOTH WORSHIP BIG BUSINESS...
NOW WHY DON'T YOU STOP THIS SILLY BICKERING, MAKE UP, AND INVADE SOME NICE MIDDLE-EAST COUNTRY? HOW ABOUT NEXT SUMMER?
BEFORE THE ELECTION?!! ARE YOU NUTS?!
SOREL

MARCH 19, 1917

TO THE PEOPLE OF BAGHDAD

IN THE NAME OF MY King, and in the name of the peoples over whom he rules, I address you as follows:

Our military operations have as their object the DEFEAT of the enemy, and the driving of him from these territories. In order to complete this task, I am charged with ABSOLUTE AND SUPREME CONTROL of all regions in which British troops operate; but our armies do not come into your cities and lands as conquerors or enemies, but as LIBERATORS. Since the days of Halaka your city and your lands have been subject to the tyranny of strangers, your palaces have fallen into ruins, your gardens have sunk in desolation, and your forefathers and yourselves have groaned in bondage. Your sons have been carried off to wars not of your seeking, YOUR WEALTH HAS BEEN STRIPPED FROM YOU by unjust men and squandered in distant places.

Since the days of Midhat, the Turks have talked of reforms, yet do not the ruins and wastes of today testify to the vanity of those promises? It is the wish not only of my King and his peoples, but also the wish of the great nations with whom he is in alliance, that you should prosper even as in the past, when your lands were fertile, when your ancestors gave to the world literature, science, and art, and when Baghdad was one of the wonders of the world.

Between your people and the dominions of my King there has been a close bond of interest. For 200 years have the merchants of Baghdad and Great Britain TRADED TOGETHER in mutual profit and friendship. On the other hand, the Germans and the Turks, who have DESPOILED you and yours, have for twenty years made Baghdad a centre of power from which to assail the power of the British and the Allies of the British in Persia and Arabia. **THEREFORE THE BRITISH GOVERNMENT CANNOT REMAIN INDIFFERENT AS TO WHAT TAKES PLACE IN YOUR COUNTRY NOW OR IN THE FUTURE,** for in duty to the interests of the British people and their Allies, the British Government cannot risk that being done in Baghdad again which has been done by the Turks and Germans during the war.

But you PEOPLE OF BAGHDAD whose commercial prosperity and whose safety from oppression and invasion must ever be a matter of the closest concern to the British Government, are NOT to understand

A proclamation issued to the inhabitants of Baghdad by Lieutenant General Sir Stanley Maude shortly after the occupation of the city by British troops

that it is the wish of the British Government to IMPOSE UPON YOU alien institutions. It is the hope of the British Government that the aspirations of your philosophers and writers shall be realised and that once again under institutions which are in consonance

THE PEOPLE OF BAGHDAD SHALL FLOURISH, ENJOYING THEIR WEALTH AND SUBSTANCE

with their sacred laws and their racial ideals. In Hedjaz the Arabs have expelled the Turks and Germans who oppressed them and proclaimed the SHERIF HUSSEIN as their King, and his Lordship rules in independence and freedom, and is the ally of the nations who are fighting against the power of Turkey and Germany; so, indeed, are the noble Arabs, the Lords of Koweyt, Nejd, and Asir.

Many noble Arabs have perished in the cause of Arab freedom, at the hands of those alien rulers, the Turks, who oppressed them. It is the determination of the Government of Great Britain and the great Powers allied to Great Britain that THESE NOBLE ARABS shall not have suffered in vain. It is the hope and desire of the British people and the nations in alliance with them that the Arab race may rise once more to greatness and renown among the peoples of the earth, and that it shall bind itself together to this end in unity and concord.

O

PEOPLE OF BAGHDAD REMEMBER that for twenty-six generations you have suffered under STRANGE TYRANTS who have ever endeavoured to set one Arab house against another in order that they might profit by your dissensions. This policy is abhorrent to Great Britain and her Allies, for there can be neither peace nor prosperity where there is enmity and misgovernment. Therefore I am commanded to invite you, through your nobles and elders and representatives, to participate in the management of your civil affairs in collaboration with the political representatives of Great Britain who accompany the British Army, so that you may be united with your kinsmen in North, East, South, and West in realising the ASPIRATIONS OF YOUR RACE.

PENTAGRAM NYC

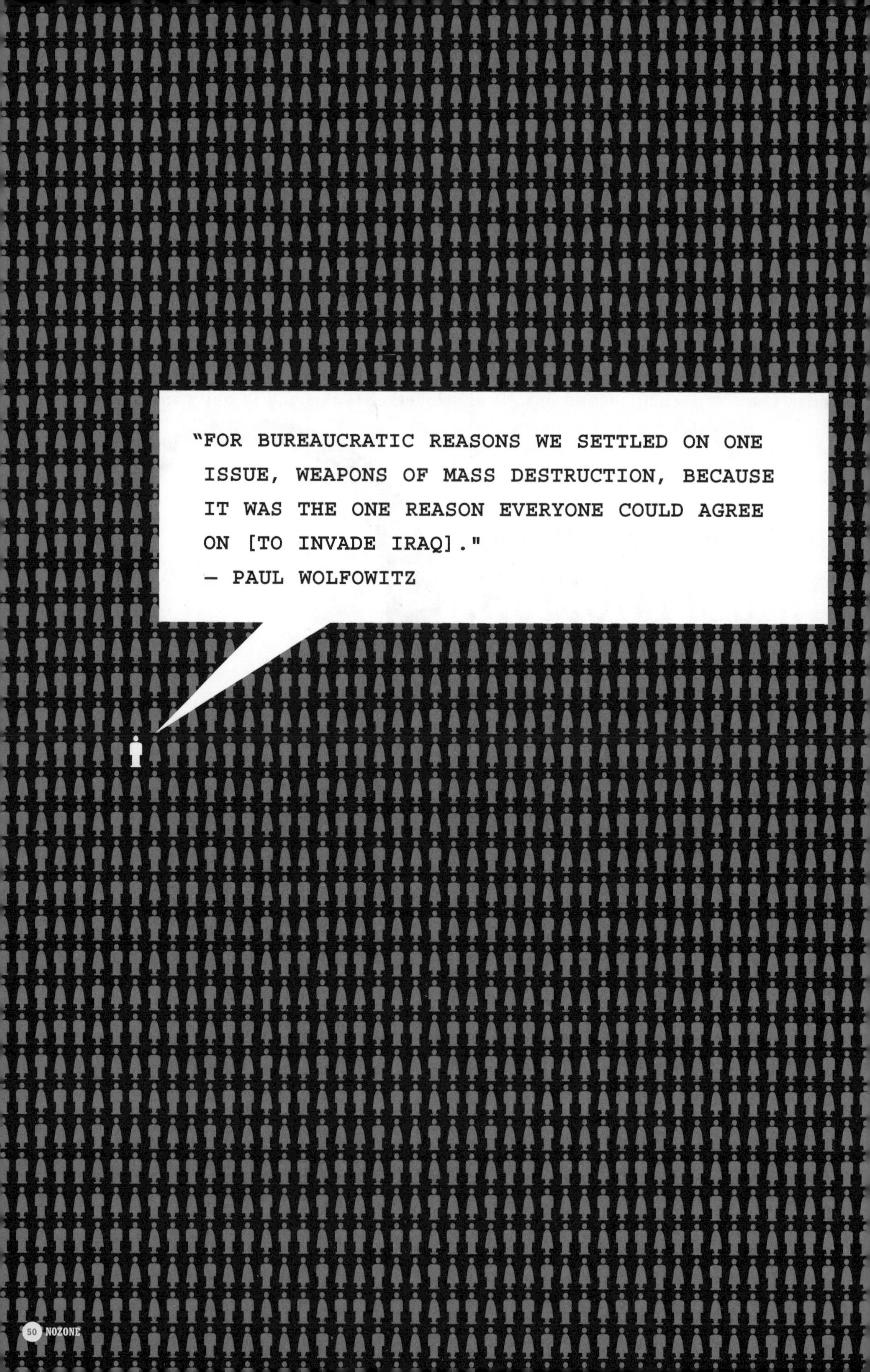
"FOR BUREAUCRATIC REASONS WE SETTLED ON ONE ISSUE, WEAPONS OF MASS DESTRUCTION, BECAUSE IT WAS THE ONE REASON EVERYONE COULD AGREE ON [TO INVADE IRAQ]."
– PAUL WOLFOWITZ

DISNEY

CBS
AOL
WB
FOX
CNN
CLEAR
NEW YORK POST

THE EAGLE HAS LANDED (again)

Official Seal of The United States

Official Seal of Iraq

"HISTORICAL DATA SHOW A STRONG CORRELATION BETWEEN U.S. INVOLVEMENT IN INTERNATIONAL SITUATIONS AND AN INCREASE IN TERRORIST ATTACKS AGAINST THE UNITED STATES."
– DEFENSE SCIENCE BOARD

... we need an imperialist foreign policy to provoke anti-Americanism ...
... we need anti-Americanism to provoke terrorist attacks on American targets ...
... we need terrorist attacks to have a war on terrorism ...
... we need a war on terrorism to justify an imperialist foreign policy...
CIRCLE OF CYNICISM

CONQUER THE UNIVERSE
with
CAPTAIN J. STAR!
GREATEST HERO AND SALESMAN OF THE A.R.C. INTER-GALACTIC SHOPPING EMPIRE!
ASK. RECEIVE. CONSUME
Hurrah!
I aspire to be just like the Captain!
Me too!
I AM Captain Star!
ARC
CONTENTMENT through CONSUMPTION

LOOK!
We've discovered ANOTHER NEW PLANET!
DAY AFTER DAY NEW PLANETS ARE ADDED TO THE A.R.C. CUSTOMER DATABASE.
I'll name this planet after you, Captain. As usual.
Carry on, First Officer... (YAWN).
UGH! I've stepped in a pool of slime!
No ordinary slime, Captain. That slime is the local inhabitants.
They must have come to watch the naming ceremony.
IMPERIALISTS!
LACKEYS OF EVIL!
CAPITALIST SCUM!
I wonder what they're saying?
DIRTY COLONIALIST!
They're saying nothing, Captain. Primitive lifeforms like these don't possess language.
The sound they're making is merely waste gas escaping.
Poo!
POP! HISS!
So... No point in trying to trade with them?
They wouldn't know a vacuum flask from a garden umbrella, Captain.
Poor fools!
They'd probably taste good in a sandwich, though, Captain.
Good idea, Navigator. I'm feeling a little peckish.
SHORTLY...
Hmm. The alien filling seems to be consuming the bread!!
CHOMP! CRUNCH!
GUZZLE... MUNCH... CHOMP...
TRANSLATION:
Delicious!
Yummy!
We must give something in exchange!
SOON.
Well I never, Captain!
What?
BELCH!
These amoeba have generated FUEL as a waste-product of eating the stale bread!
Well, well...
It appears we CAN do business with these little fellows after all, Scarlette.
Not 'fellows' Captain. Amoeba are sexless, single-celled organisms.
LATER, AFTER LOADING THE NEW FUEL.
I wonder what they'd be saying right now – if they could speak.
DOWN BELOW...
HAIL, Captain Star!
HAIL!
We love you and worship you! RULE us!
COLONIALISM through COMMERCE!

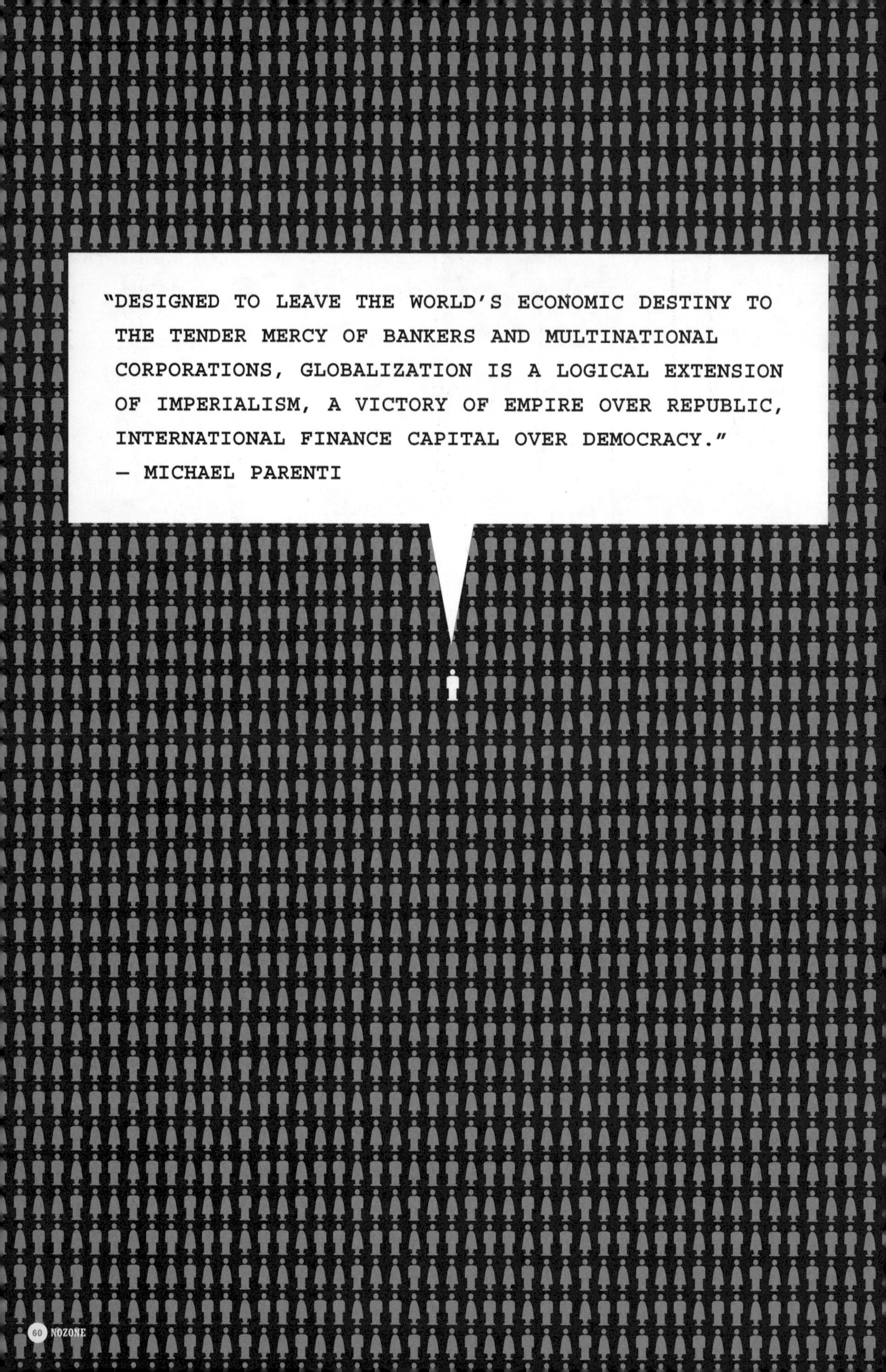
"DESIGNED TO LEAVE THE WORLD'S ECONOMIC DESTINY TO THE TENDER MERCY OF BANKERS AND MULTINATIONAL CORPORATIONS, GLOBALIZATION IS A LOGICAL EXTENSION OF IMPERIALISM, A VICTORY OF EMPIRE OVER REPUBLIC, INTERNATIONAL FINANCE CAPITAL OVER DEMOCRACY."
– MICHAEL PARENTI

GLOBALIZED

1 "Globalization" sounds optimistic. It suggests a movement toward the end of nationalism, racism, and other things that divide us.

2 It brings to mind compassion, peace, and a celebration of any-thing that can bring us all together – an awareness of the world as a single living organism.

3 But "globalization" also brings to mind phrases like "multi-national corp-oration."

4 A company from America, reg-istered in Malaysia, with offices in Frankfurt, and product dis-tribution on all five continents.

5 Mega markets.

6 Mega supply.

7 Mega demand.

8 Globalization skims along the surface with light-ning-speed and awesome effi-ciency.

9 A Coca-Cola sign in Beijing, a pair of Nikes on the feet of a Zimbabwean, a cash-machine half way up the Matterhorn.

10 Global-ization may sound sporty – but it's not a game.

11 Because a person at a computer on Wall Street can control the destiny of another person in Peru.

12 Because globalization is changing the shape of the planet from a sphere into a giant pyramid, with the super rich at the top and the super-poor at the bottom.

13 Because the more triumphantly "global" the world becomes, the more insignificant and alone we will become.

14 BUT eat a tomato grown in Palestine and you are global-izing...

15 ...learn another lang-uage and speak to someone in it, and you are globalizing...

16 ...emit fewer fluoro-carbons, and you are global-izing.

17 In fact, almost anything you do can be thought of globally.

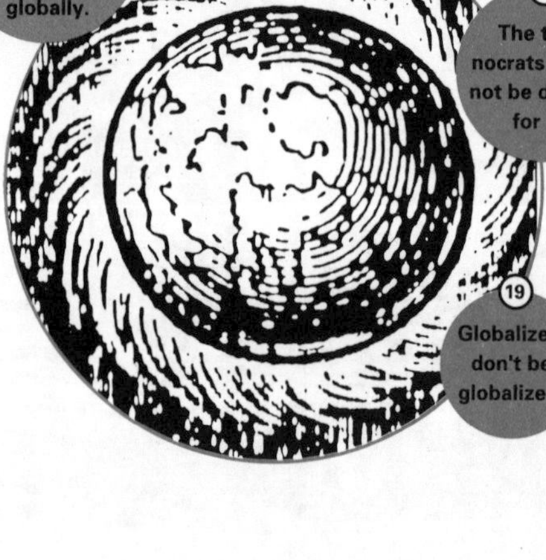

18 The tech-nocrats should not be doing it for us.

19 Globalize – don't be globalized.

"NOT ONLY IS THE CASE FOR PRESIDENT BUSH'S 'OPINION' THAT 'FREE TRADE IS GOOD FOR BOTH WEALTHY AND IMPOVERISHED NATIONS' EMPIRICALLY FEEBLE; THERE IS PLENTY OF EVIDENCE THAT RICH COUNTRIES, STARTING WITH THE UNITED STATES, HAVE NO INTENTION OF PLAYING BY THE TRADE RULES AND STRICTURES THEY FOIST ON POORER, WEAKER COUNTRIES AS 'A SINGLE SUSTAINABLE MODEL'... THEIRS IS NOT AN IDEOLOGY OF FREEDOM OR DEMOCRACY. IT IS A SYSTEM OF CONTROL. IT IS AN ECONOMICS OF EMPIRE."

— WILLIAM FINNEGAN

http://
members.
aol.
com/sunstar
253/
images
/globe05
.gif

http://
www.
expressair
marine
.com/
adi_24hrs
_
over_NA_ sm
.
gif

http
://www.
ahumanbeing.
co.uk/LuckyDip/
spinningworlds/
continents
.gif

http:
//www
.national.
com/globe
.gif

http:
//noaa.
gov/ert
.gif

http
://www.
delta.
edu/culture/
GLOBE2
.GIF

http
://trek
kies.org/
spin1.gi
f

http
:
/ /
www.
bek.no/images/
gif
/
allanimated/
globe
/
earth2
.
gi
f

http
://users.
hol
.
gr/~
andreas
/
images/
earth
1.gif

http
://xs4a
ll.nl/g.
gif

http:
//hum.
amu.edu
.pl/~zbzw/
ani74.g
if

http:
//hum.
amu.edu
.pl/
~zbzw/
ani96.gif

http
: / /
w
w w
.
chloesevigny
.
com/
graphics_coolstuff/
anims/
earth_an
.
gif

http:
//whale.
wheelock
.edu/spin
.gif

http
://
www.
colleenshannon.
com
/
globe.gif

http://
www
.mcps.
org
/
admin/
htmltips/
gan
im5b.
gif

http:
//amu.e
du.pl/a
.gif

http:
/ /
www.freenet
.
hamilton.
on.ca
/~ad048/
earth
.
gif

http:/
/hum.
edu/~zbzw/
globe
/ani8.
gif

Online Rotating Globes

The first spinning globe animated gif appeared online in 1995. Since then, it has appeared on servers across the world, possibly becoming the de facto logo of the Internet. Presented are a selection of spinning globes collected from geographically dispersed websites.

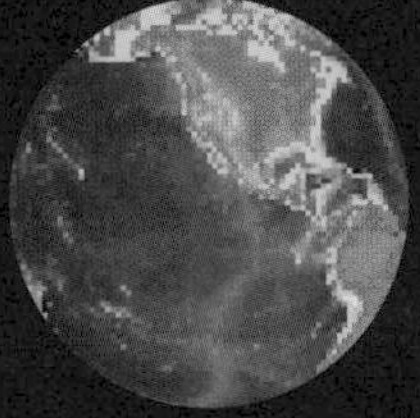

UNITED STATES

MOROCCO

ITALY

ALTARS TO THE EMPIRE

Check your wallet. If you are carrying an ATM card then you are a fully registered member of the empire. Armed with just this piece of plastic, and your "secret password," of course, you have the privilege of being able to go to any corner of the globe and tap into the largest, mightiest, most universal financial system ever to exist. After paying your respects at the altar of your choice, you are invited to take your cash and – if you wish to practice the only form of service fully recognized by our system – spend it. — JESSE GORDON

AUSTRALIA

INDIA

ELAND

SPAIN

ANGLADESH

ERMANY

GREECE

SWITZERLAND

RUSSIA

ANADA

FINLAND

ICELAND

JAPAN

HINA

SOUTH KOREA

DAM

China has undertaken its most ambitious construction project since the Great Wall. The Three Gorges Dam on the Yangtze River will be the world's largest; at 1.5 miles wide and 600 feet tall, it will create a virtual inland sea more than 400 miles long.

Controversy has arisen concerning the environmental impact and human rights violations associated with the $25 billion project. Through an involuntary, government-run "resettlement" program, a million people are being relocated. Many farming families are being moved onto much less fertile land. Other families are being forced to change their professions without being taught new job skills. The resulting water pollution, deforestation, and erosion are expected to alter the current ecosystem and threaten the habitats of many endangered species, including the Yangtze dolphin (pop. 200), the Chinese sturgeon, the Chinese alligator, the Chinese tiger, the Siberian crane, and the giant panda. After the Tiananmen Square massacre in June 1989, however, the government forbade public debate of the dam, accused naysayers of ignorance or intent to undermine the regime, and imprisoned journalist Dai Qing and other famous critics.

(1) This is a Chinese tourist posing in front of the Xiao Sanxia or "Three Little Gorges." When the dam's reservoir reaches its maximum height in 2009, the Three Little Gorges will be completely submerged. As the dam nears completion, hundreds of tourist boats make the three-day trip up and down the Yangtze from Chongqing to Wuhan. Eager for a last glimpse at some of China's most precious natural wonders and ancient sites, tourists stop along the riverbanks in "ghost cities" such as Yunyang and Dachang. More than 120 cities and towns will be drowned along with countless historic artifacts. Red-lettered signs are painted on houses and temples marking the water levels of the coming flood.

The tourist boats are dirty and makeshift, with rats and karaoke bars. Most of the Chinese who can afford the trip are proud, and dress accordingly. Men wear suits, and women wear dresses and heels, donning the color-coded baseball hats of their tour group. This man has bought a pair of green, plastic binoculars from a local souvenir hawker.

(2) In my room on the tourist boat, I bought this ceramic plate at a souvenir stand on the riverbank. It depicts portraits of various Chinese generals since the cultural revolution. I imagined eating spaghetti off of it. I mailed it back to the states from Wuhan, and it arrived in a million pieces.

(3) This is Dragon Gate Gorge, the entrance to the Three Little Gorges. The unfinished bridge in the distance will eventually lurk inches below the water level.

The government's stated intentions for the dam project are flood control, hydroelectric power generation, and increased navigation potential on the river. Given the evidence that the dam may not achieve these goals, many opponents wonder why the government presses on with the project. The conclusion seems to be that the primary motivation is political. The world's largest hydroelectric dam will confirm China's technological prowess and the superiority of socialism.

(1)

(2)

(3)

PAID ADVERTISEMENT

PAID ADVERTISEMENT

☐ **YES!** FREE US WITH YOUR FIREPOWER AND FRANCHISES!

☐ **NO.** (OR DO WE REALLY HAVE ANY CHOICE IN THE MATTER?)

COUNTRY: ________

DESPOT: ________

NATIONAL RESOURCES OF ANY CONSIDERABLE FINANCIAL VALUE:

____

____

____

MAIL TO:
DICK CHENEY, USA

WEAPONS
OF MASS DESTRUCTION

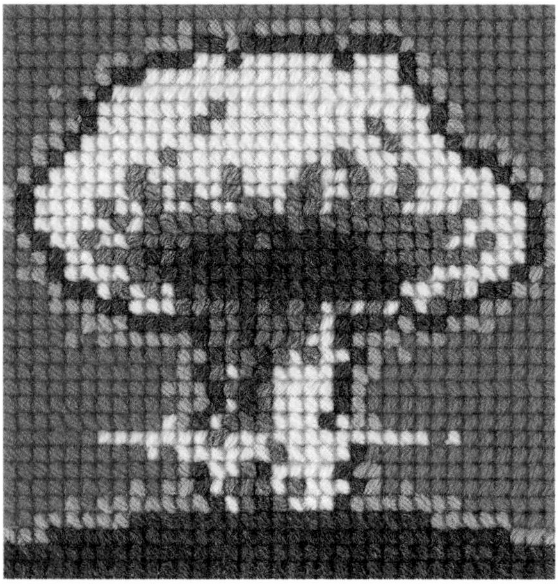

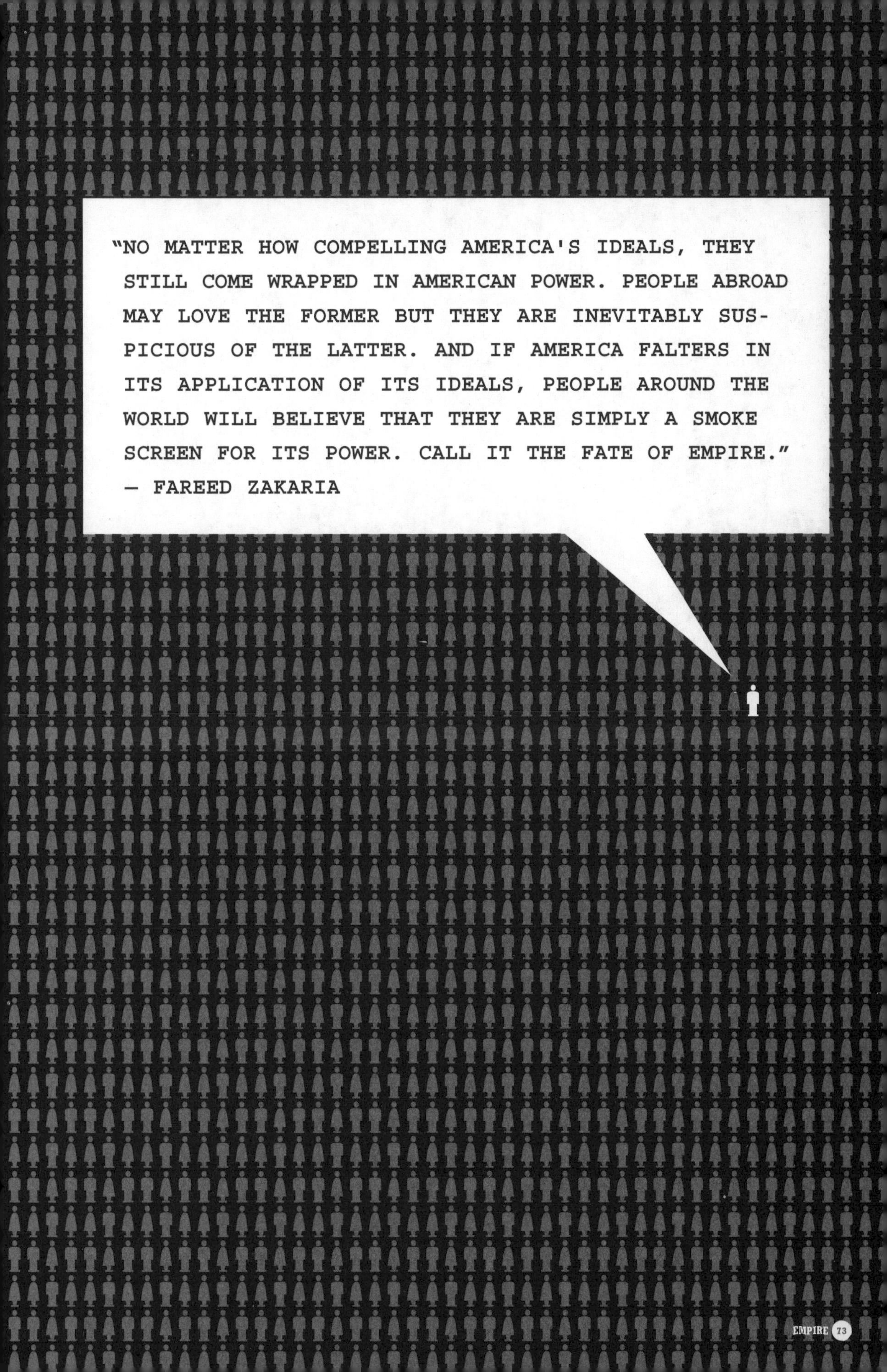
"NO MATTER HOW COMPELLING AMERICA'S IDEALS, THEY STILL COME WRAPPED IN AMERICAN POWER. PEOPLE ABROAD MAY LOVE THE FORMER BUT THEY ARE INEVITABLY SUSPICIOUS OF THE LATTER. AND IF AMERICA FALTERS IN ITS APPLICATION OF ITS IDEALS, PEOPLE AROUND THE WORLD WILL BELIEVE THAT THEY ARE SIMPLY A SMOKE SCREEN FOR ITS POWER. CALL IT THE FATE OF EMPIRE."
— FAREED ZAKARIA

"WE NEED A COMMON ENEMY TO UNITE US."
– CONDOLEEZA RICE, NATIONAL SECURITY ADVISOR

tURF
WAR

tURF WAR

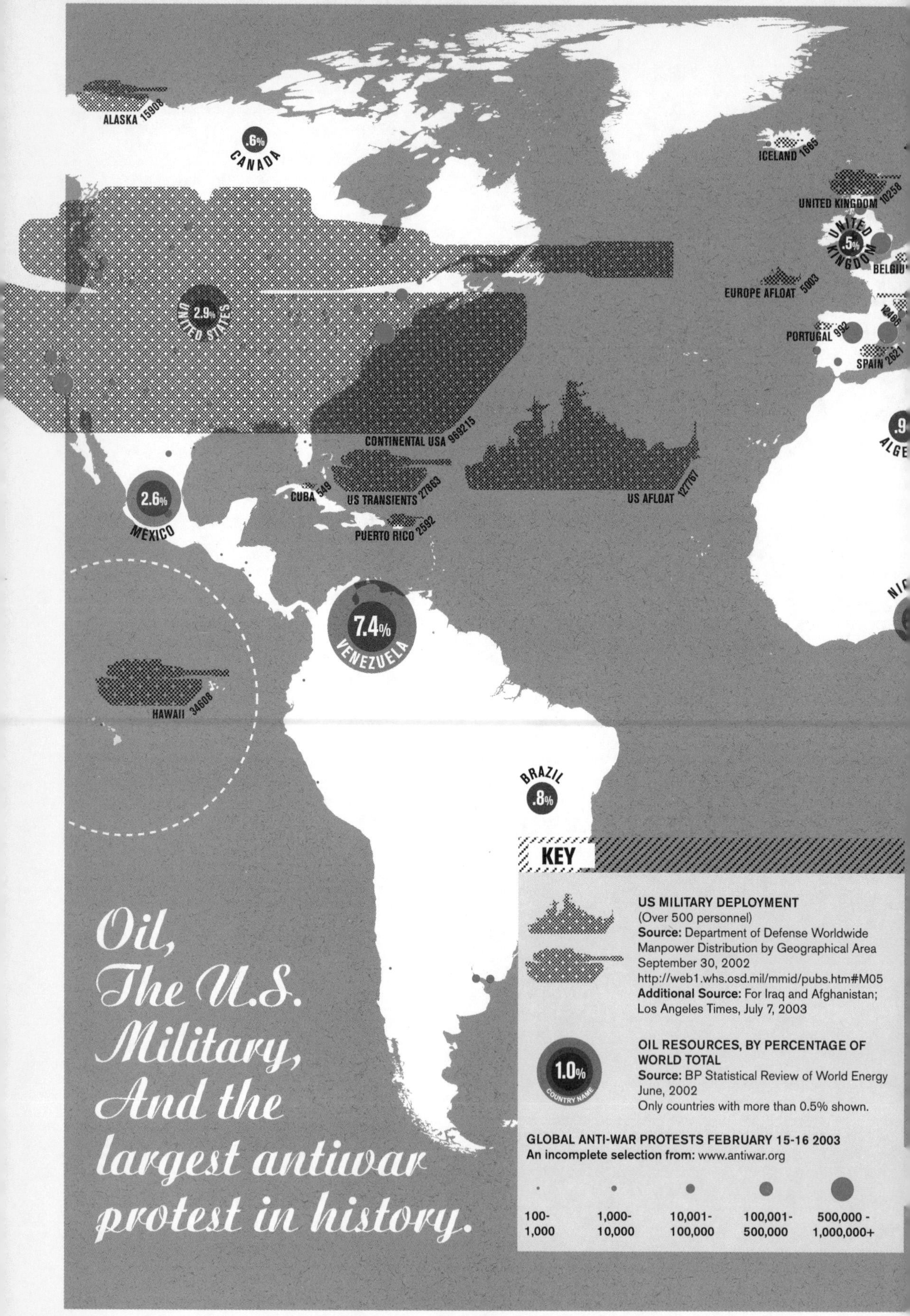

Oil, The U.S. Military, And the largest antiwar protest in history.

KEY

US MILITARY DEPLOYMENT
(Over 500 personnel)
Source: Department of Defense Worldwide Manpower Distribution by Geographical Area September 30, 2002
http://web1.whs.osd.mil/mmid/pubs.htm#M05
Additional Source: For Iraq and Afghanistan; Los Angeles Times, July 7, 2003

OIL RESOURCES, BY PERCENTAGE OF WORLD TOTAL
1.0% COUNTRY NAME
Source: BP Statistical Review of World Energy June, 2002
Only countries with more than 0.5% shown.

GLOBAL ANTI-WAR PROTESTS FEBRUARY 15-16 2003
An incomplete selection from: www.antiwar.org

100-1,000 | 1,000-10,000 | 10,001-100,000 | 100,001-500,000 | 500,000 - 1,000,000+

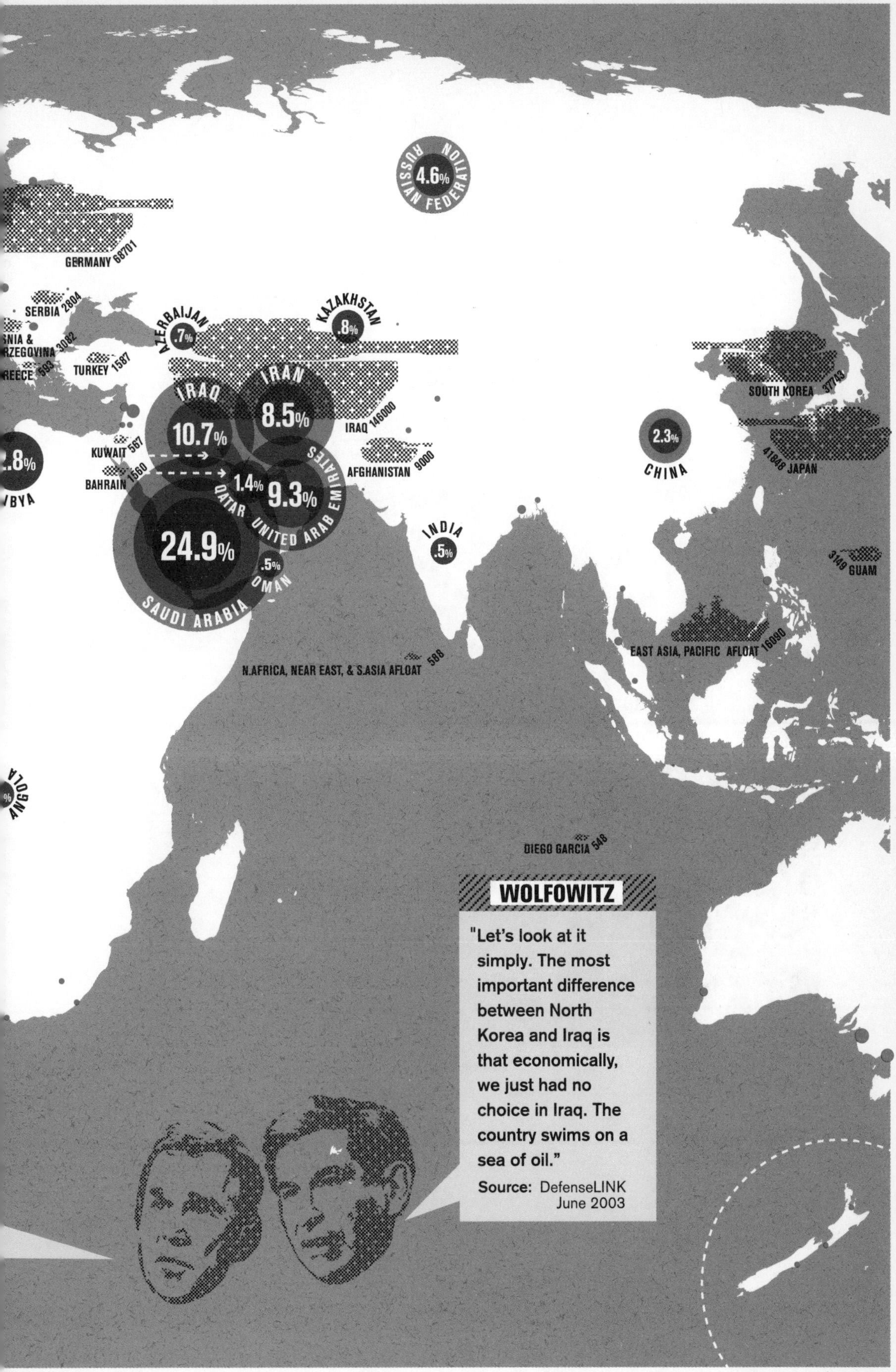

WOLFOWITZ

"Let's look at it simply. The most important difference between North Korea and Iraq is that economically, we just had no choice in Iraq. The country swims on a sea of oil."

Source: DefenseLINK June 2003

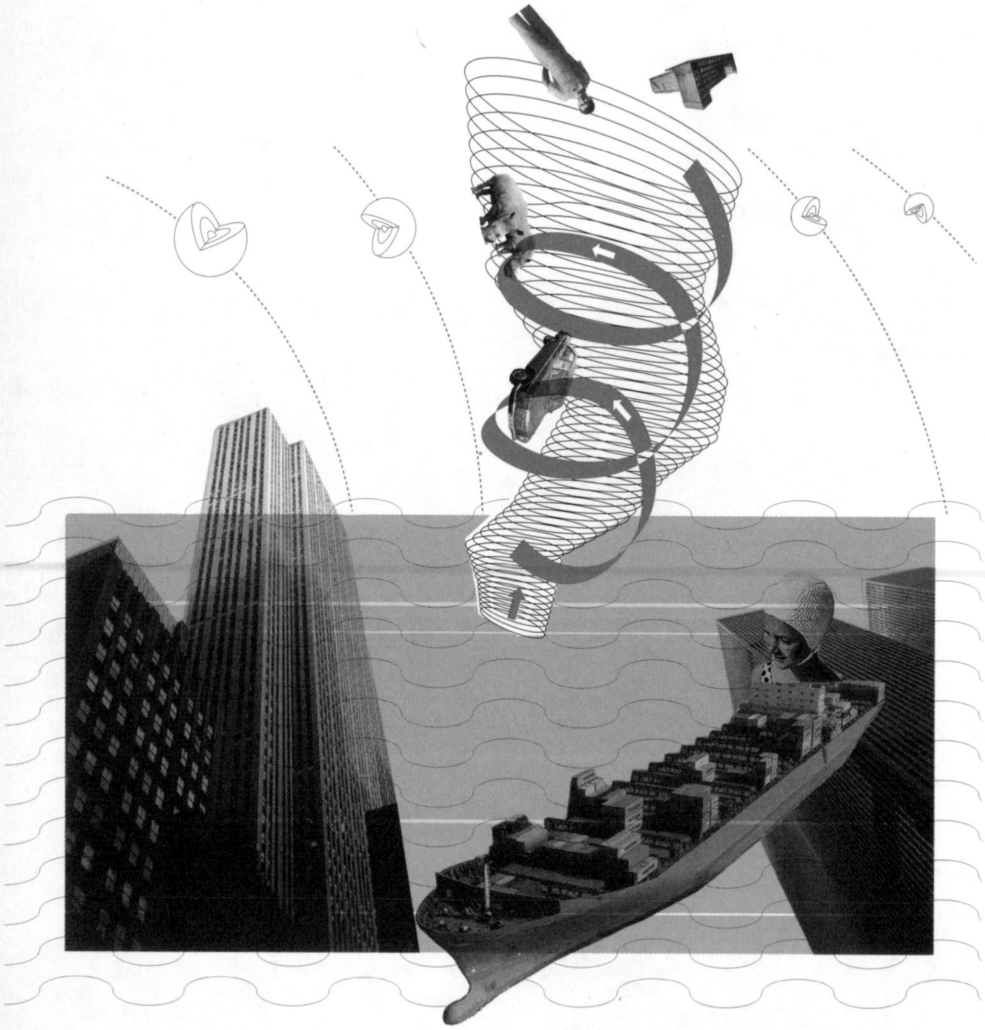

S.U.V.S AXLES of EVIL
THEOCRAT SAND ROVER
GRAND DICTATOR KJ-IL
SADDAMBASSADOR
OR Chariots of the GOOD
IMPERIAL TROOPER
HOMELAND DEFENDER
CRUSADER CRUISE COUNTRY

AMERICAN
LEWIS LAPHAM TALKS ABOUT EMPIRE

INTERVIEW BY ELIZABETH AMON | ILLUSTRATION BY CHRISTOPH NIEMANN

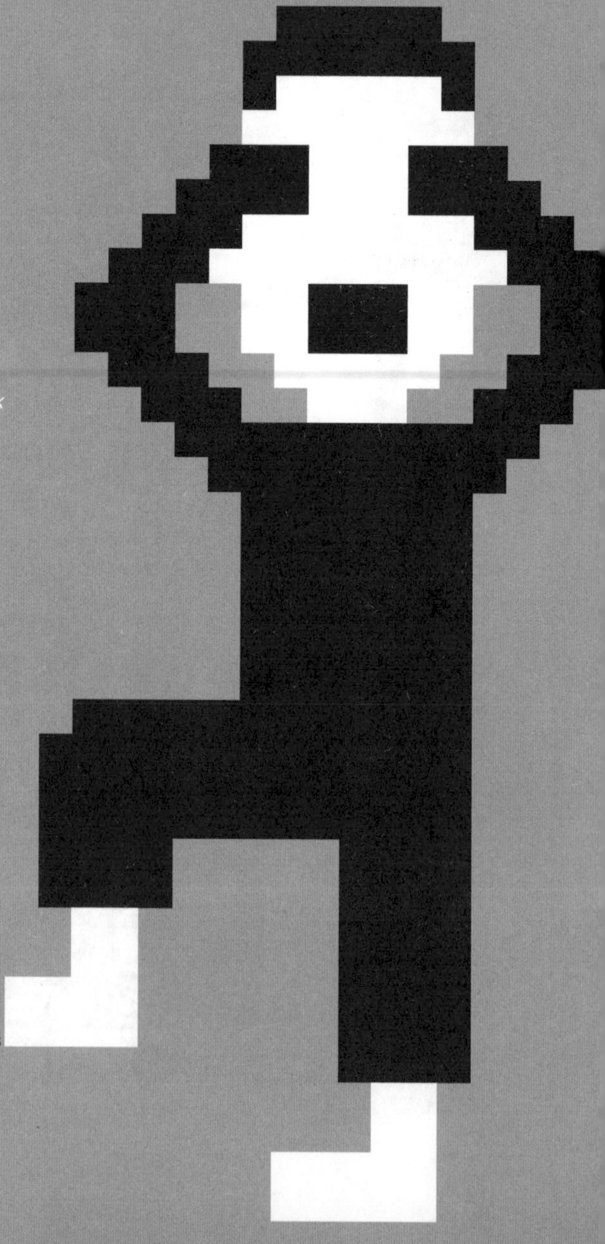

ELIZABETH AMON: The word "empire" has been widely used by the media to both positively and negatively characterize post–September 11 America. As the editor of *Harper's* magazine, you've overseen the publication in recent months of articles titled "The Economics of Empire," "The Romance of Empire," and "The Course of Empire."

And you've peppered your monthly columns with references to the American empire. You've linked Congress's joint resolution giving Bush the power to go to war in Iraq to the Roman practice of enthroning dictators. You've compared the American empire to the 1,000-year Byzantine Empire, which produced no noteworthy statesmen. You've compared the *New York Times Magazine* coverage of the American empire to a fashion show. You've disparaged the moral argument for an American empire that portrays Saddam Hussein as a foe as fearsome as Hitler or Stalin. And you've denounced the hypocrisy of an American empire that, while toting arms, is touting peace on earth and good will toward men.

Do you see the American empire as a definable entity? Is this just a new word for "American imperialism" or is there a difference?

LEWIS LAPHAM: I use the word "empire" in numerous ways, and most of the time I'm talking about delusions of grandeur: the notion that a single autocratic state – whether Rome in the first century B.C., Spain in the seventeenth century, Britain in the nineteenth century, or Berlin in the years 1936–45 – can form a single seat of power governing the whole world. Usually, my use of the word is in terms of what I take to be the dreaming fantasy of the minds of our political overlords in Washington – people who sit in handsomely furnished air-conditioned offices, with the latest up-to-the-minute technology, maps with little flags marking the

OLIGARCHY

positions of fleets and armies. They sit there thinking that somehow they can impose an imperial order, they can tell the rest of the world how to behave and what to do, and they can teach manners, whether to the restless natives of the Alta Plano or the newly emerged of Eastern Europe. And I think many of those notions are vain. I don't think that it is possible to run the world as if it were a corporation.

EA: Given George W. Bush's high approval ratings and the fact that the administration's actions have been popularly and legislatively supported, is the American empire validated as a democratic imperial project or do you see it as an oligarchy?

LL: I think it's being run as an oligarchy with a sense of what Washington people like to call "unilateralism" – reserving Washington the right to decide which treaties to sign, which nations to identify as criminals or members of the axis of evil, and to do as it wishes with regard to the international treaties of law, environment, land mines, and weapons, all of which Washington recognizes or ignores as it pleases.

I look at the Congress and I see, for the most part, the same class of people more or less indistinguishable from one another. They tend to be lawyers and professional politicians or they tend to be rich men who can afford the price of a campaign. Increasingly over the last twenty or thirty years, it's become almost a matter of inheritance. It's not only the Bush father and son; since 1974 we haven't had a presidential election without a Dole or a Gore or a Bush. When it comes time to think about who might be put up for public office, it's usually the same relatively brief list of names.

Part of that is because we also have in this country what is called a "donor class" (the phrase is Michael Lind's). There are between 200,000 and 300,000 entities, individuals, trade associations, and lobbying groups that put up by far the bulk of the money for all of the campaigns. As these campaigns become more and more expensive, only the people who pass the board of review, the tribunal of the donor class, are chosen as candidates – that is, by the country's moneyed interests. There is no argument with that. You saw what happened to Ralph Nadar when he tried to go around that obstacle in 2000. He didn't even get five percent of the vote. Only if backed by that kind of cash will a candidate be taken seriously by the media. Only in the last six weeks has the media begun to take Howard Dean seriously, not because of what he's saying but because of the money he's been collecting. And I don't care what surface reform is based on campaign finance reform, that is the way the system works.

The oligarchy, within the Bush administration, is like polo or golf. I don't see a large enthusiasm for it on the part of the broad mass of the American people. And as you can see, we are beginning to lose. I think fifty American soldiers have been killed since the war was officially declared at an end on May 1 [as of July 29, 2003], and already you begin to see mutterings of discontent, people asking why. That's a very small number of people compared to the number of legionnaires the Romans were prepared to lose in an afternoon's work in Gaul.

EA: Do you think the idea of empire emerged after the terrorist attacks of September 11?

LL: It's always been in the minds of certain American interests. In the current issue of the magazine [August 2003] I wrote in my column about a book Walter Karp wrote [*Politics of War*]. Karp's point – and I think he makes it very persuasively – is that the notion of empire is present in the nineteenth century.

There's a big painting titled *Westward the Course of Empire Takes its Way* on the west wall of the Capital. In it a figure, one of a group of settlers, points to the horizon. So the notion of a continental empire, or a manifest destiny, "54°40′ or fight" [the slogan for the American campaign to claim the territory of Oregon from the British], the notion that the United States must run from sea to shining sea is very present in the

nineteenth century. I'm not saying that everybody subscribed to it but certainly there were those who did, such as John Charles Frémont, the great "Pathfinder," and his father-in-law, Senator Thomas Hart Benton of Missouri. At the end of the nineteenth century, the idea of world empire came to the fore in the minds of the Republican oligarchy in power in Washington and Wall Street in order to distract attention from the populist movement that was then threatening to unsettle the status quo.

You can see it's very clear over our history – the Spanish American War puts an end to the populist movement, our involvement in World War I puts an end to the progressive movement, World War II puts an end to the New Deal. I'm not saying we didn't have any choice about World War II, but we did have a choice about both the Spanish American War and our engagement in World War I. In World War I, ninety percent of the American people were against the American entrance on the side of the allies. Our appearance in the war was very artfully arranged by Woodrow Wilson and some of the moneyed interests. Certainly all of Lyndon B. Johnson's hopes for rebuilding the United States and founding within it a great society were pretty well washed out to sea by the Vietnam War and by the Cold War, of which it was a part.

Within an empire, one tends to have subjects, as opposed to a republic, which supposedly has citizens. And so the making of an empire, the making of a large, nation-state, necessarily entails a diminishing of civil liberties and civil rights. Again, most empires are always at war. If one lives in a society that is always at war, then freedom of expression becomes potentially dangerous. You might give aid and comfort to the enemy. Dissent becomes even more unpopular than in times of ease, peace, and prosperity, and one gives up a good deal of one's own freedom in order to participate in the glory of empire. This is a contrary notion from the one of a democratic republic in which the greatest glory is the success and full flowering of the individual rather than the success and triumph of the state. Better that the citizen should write a poem, paint a picture, invent a machine, build a family, make something useful or beautiful, make something of his or her life. It's a plural narrative in a democracy and a republic. In an empire it's the story of the state. I love the United States for its freedoms, not for its armies, its fleets, its victories, and so on. It's a different way of defining oneself.

EA: Your column on Karp's book, pointing out the parallels between our time and the state of politics one hundred years ago, suggests that little has changed. What needs to be done to make a change?

LL: It's an argument, a dialectic. Many people have put it well in opposition to the Mexican War, for example. Perhaps the best is Henry David Thoreau in *Civil Disobedience*. He writes of going to jail as a response to refusing to pay taxes. His refusal was based, in part, on his objection to the Mexican War and to the notion of empire. As a Congressman Abraham Lincoln expressed the same kind of objection to the Mexican War in the 1840s and as a result lost his seat in Congress and thought he was never going to get back into government.

John Quincy Adams, when he was Secretary of State in the 1820s, is another. There was the newly emergent American nation, having defeated the British in the war of 1812, thinking of sending the navy to the west coast of

South America to rid Columbia through Chile of the Spanish viceroys. Adams argued against it. He said, "America goes not abroad in search of monsters to destroy" because if we do that we bind ourselves in all of the intrigue, ambition, deceit, and wasted money that that kind of imperial thinking entails. "We may conquer the world but we will lose our soul." It's a magnificent quote.

That argument was also made by Mark Twain in a wonderful debate in 1900. Twain, then close to the end of his life, a grand old man in a white suit and white hair, was vice president of the Anti-Imperial League and led the objections to the American occupation in the Philippines as a consequence of the Spanish American War. He was very outspoken on this subject. Twain's writings on the cruelty of empire and the stupidity of military conquest are truly wonderful to read. He had the debate in the old Madison Square Garden with the apostle of empire who was then the best-selling author in the United States – Winston Churchill, who was then twenty-three or twenty-four and had just made a miraculous escape from the Boar War, had written a book about his daring do on the South African Veldt, and was the toast of New York.

These same kinds of arguments went on during the Vietnam War. There was a wonderful parallel at Yale in the late thirties – the class of '38 or '39 – between two best friends and, I think, roommates and certainly the two most brilliant students in the class. One is Dave Dellinger (of the Chicago 7, a group of anti–Vietnam War activists) and the other is Walt Rostow (presidential adviser and proponent of Vietnam), and they went in absolutely opposite directions.

So the argument is always there at some level. At the moment it's very submerged, although it's not as submerged as you would think reading the *New York Times* and watching network television. If you look at moveon.org and read a lot of the civil liberties union news, or Nat Hentoff or Alex Cockburn, there seem to be a lot of people objecting to the imperial notion. But their voices don't really make it into the mainstream. The mainstream is filled with people like Michael Ignatieff, author of "The American Empire: Get Used to It" [published in the *New York Times Magazine*, January 5, 2003] or Thomas L. Friedman. The American intelligentsia who are on the commanding heights of the American discourse at the moment are pro-empire, pro-American power.

EA: Given that this kind of discourse has been going on for one hundred years, and yet the wars continue, do you believe continuing the argument is effective?

LL: Yes I do. There's an article on the front page of the *New York Times* today, "Centrist Democrats Want Party Not to Present Itself as Far Left." By "far left," they hardly mean far left – they're not talking about Herbert Marcuse or Karl Marx. They're simply talking about people who make a squeak of objection to the tax cuts or complain about the war. In Europe that would be considered centrist, but here it's shockingly far left. And what the Democratic Leadership Council is recommending is, shut up, go quietly, do what the money says, don't make arguments or you will be cast in the pit, painted as a radical, and identified with Bob Dylan. If you do that we'll lose – this is what they're saying. The truth of the matter is the DLC doesn't care whether or not it loses because it will stay in power. It won't have as much power but it still will have a place at the table.

There's no energy in our politics at the moment. I don't know what you do about that. Clearly it's a question I've been asked more than once and I don't have a good answer, but I keep struggling. I keep trying.

EA: And what of Marcuse's argument that democracy permits dissent, and the only way to make real changes is to work outside the system?

LL: It's not only what Marcuse was saying thirty years ago, it's also what Marshall McLuhan was saying thirty years ago. With electronic media, it's very difficult to come up with a coherent politics because the electronic media are themselves incoherent and irrational and adjusted to the voice of the demagogue rather than for the use of enlightenment. It's very hard to make a coherent political argument on television. First of all there's a time constraint. Second of all, the language that one must use on television – I couldn't talk this way

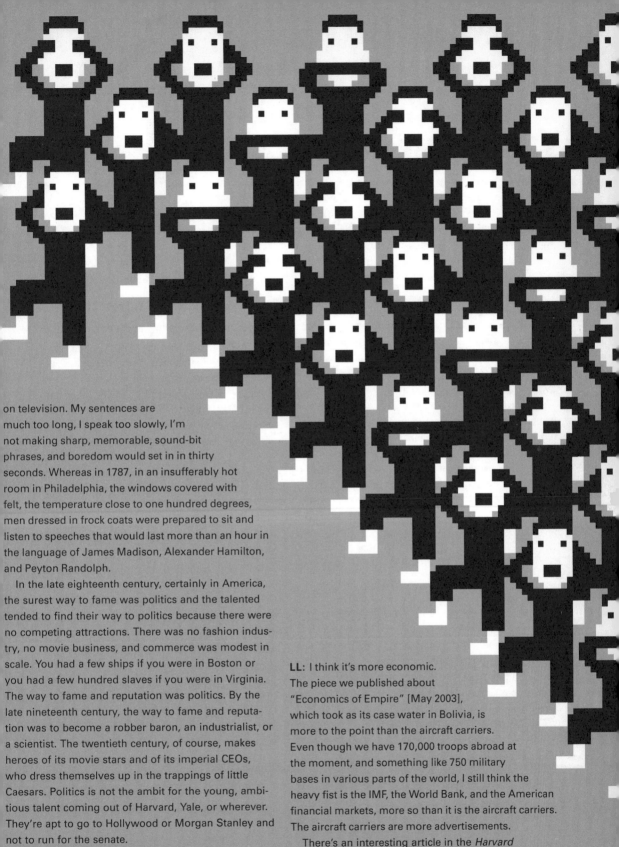

on television. My sentences are much too long, I speak too slowly, I'm not making sharp, memorable, sound-bit phrases, and boredom would set in in thirty seconds. Whereas in 1787, in an insufferably hot room in Philadelphia, the windows covered with felt, the temperature close to one hundred degrees, men dressed in frock coats were prepared to sit and listen to speeches that would last more than an hour in the language of James Madison, Alexander Hamilton, and Peyton Randolph.

In the late eighteenth century, certainly in America, the surest way to fame was politics and the talented tended to find their way to politics because there were no competing attractions. There was no fashion industry, no movie business, and commerce was modest in scale. You had a few ships if you were in Boston or you had a few hundred slaves if you were in Virginia. The way to fame and reputation was politics. By the late nineteenth century, the way to fame and reputation was to become a robber baron, an industrialist, or a scientist. The twentieth century, of course, makes heroes of its movie stars and of its imperial CEOs, who dress themselves up in the trappings of little Caesars. Politics is not the ambit for the young, ambitious talent coming out of Harvard, Yale, or wherever. They're apt to go to Hollywood or Morgan Stanley and not to run for the senate.

EA: Do you see the American empire as essentially one of military supremacy, or is it more founded on economic power and run by supra-national corporations?

LL: I think it's more economic. The piece we published about "Economics of Empire" [May 2003], which took as its case water in Bolivia, is more to the point than the aircraft carriers. Even though we have 170,000 troops abroad at the moment, and something like 750 military bases in various parts of the world, I still think the heavy fist is the IMF, the World Bank, and the American financial markets, more so than it is the aircraft carriers. The aircraft carriers are more advertisements.

There's an interesting article in the *Harvard International Review* by Joseph Stiglitz, who, in the late 1990s, was the chief economist and senior vice president of the World Bank and was also a Nobel prize–winning economist. It points out that the way the IMF and the international financing of so-called underdeveloped countries is set up is that the lending and borrowing that goes on between the U.S. and the IMF and Brazil, Argentina, Mexico, and West Africa is set up with different structures. When underdeveloped countries lend money on $100 million dollars of value, they collect $8 million, whereas on $100 million dollars of debt they pay $18 million – so they're screwed, and that's not an accident.

The thing that would bring down the pretensions of the American empire much more rapidly than any military strike would be a decision on the part of the oil countries to denominate the price of oil in euros, or possibly the yen, instead of dollars. Because we are now able to denominate our enormous debt in our own currency, we can manipulate it. The Argentines, the Mexicans, and the Liberians all have to pay in dollars. If we had to pay in euros, we'd be in a lot of trouble, very, very quickly. And that's what will happen if the empire begins to fail, if the balloons begin to pop in the grand ballroom of the Hilton Hotel. It will be for those kinds of reasons, because we will have mismanaged our economy. It is enormous compared to the rest of the world, but still the stupidity that is up and about and abroad in Washington is equal to the task.

EA: What is the role of the media in creating American empire?

LL: The media loves the story of the empire. It thinks of itself as a function – I'm talking about the big media: the Washington talk-show circuit, the *New York Times*, the *Wall Street Journal*, *Time*, *Newsweek*, the dress circle of the American news media. I think those people think of themselves as agents and functionaries of the government rather than witnesses on behalf of the American people. I think that by and large the national news media plays the part of Polonius in *Hamlet*, full of wise saws, sound advice, terrified about its own place at court. I could also think of it as Rosencrantz and Guildenstern to use the same play, courtiers by and large dependent upon access.

EA: Yet individual reporters, at least those outside of the Washington press corps, would strenuously deny their role as a hireling of the government. Is this a parallel to the American public's comprehension of the empire building of the government?

LL: McLuhan touches on this at some length in a lot of his writing. When you get an enormous corporate media, it's a collective consciousness, which doesn't postulate a consciousness in anything in particular. And the voice of the individual is drowned in the void of the collective.

Fifteen years ago, I had a piece given to me by a big-time writer from *Time* magazine (I can't now remember his name). It was the last time I entertained a manuscript from someone like that – I should know better. We actually put this piece in type. It was about 8,000 words long. It was written in the omniscient third person in a *Time* manner. "All America wept yesterday" or "last week it rained in America," to use it as the image of the death of a dog or a movie star. Anyway, the guy got to the end of the manuscript and in the last paragraph he permitted himself the phrase, "So and so and so, I think." And then when he saw that in the galley, he changed it to read, "Millions of people say." That's really all you have to know about *Time* magazine.

I was a newspaper reporter for four years, first for the *San Francisco Examiner* and then for the old *Harold Tribune* in New York. I learned very quickly what was going to make page one and what wasn't. And God help you that you put anything in the first person. They don't allow people to use the first person until they've become so tame, like David Brooks or Tom Friedman, that they know they're not going to say anything out of line. If you stay in that omniscient third, that's the problem.

Tom Wicker said this some years ago in a forum we had in *Harper's* magazine: the national press considers itself a gentleman's club. Dan Rather, in one of his bursts of candor, said in the same conversation: what we have is a suck-up press. And he's a man who ought to know. Henry Adams said it as long ago as the 1890s: the press is the hireling of the moneyed interests. And that's what the big media's about. It's there to reassure its audiences and to present the good news. America is a wonder of an admiring world. Our armies are invincible, our artists capable of masterpieces, our people the happiest and freest who ever walked the earth. That is the message and the big media is by definition an advertising media. They are there to move the product, and part of the product is its own magnificence.

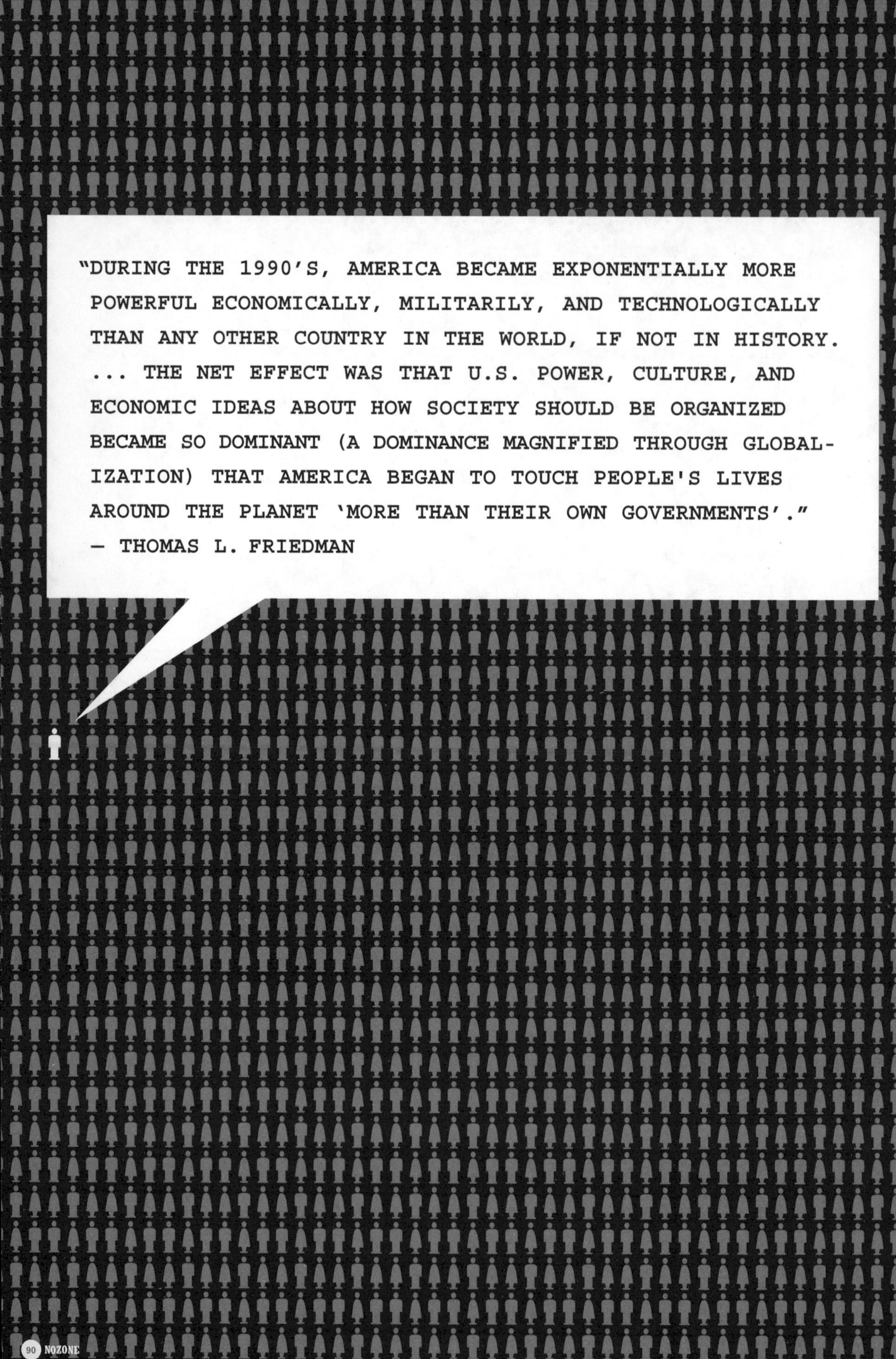
"DURING THE 1990'S, AMERICA BECAME EXPONENTIALLY MORE POWERFUL ECONOMICALLY, MILITARILY, AND TECHNOLOGICALLY THAN ANY OTHER COUNTRY IN THE WORLD, IF NOT IN HISTORY. ... THE NET EFFECT WAS THAT U.S. POWER, CULTURE, AND ECONOMIC IDEAS ABOUT HOW SOCIETY SHOULD BE ORGANIZED BECAME SO DOMINANT (A DOMINANCE MAGNIFIED THROUGH GLOBALIZATION) THAT AMERICA BEGAN TO TOUCH PEOPLE'S LIVES AROUND THE PLANET 'MORE THAN THEIR OWN GOVERNMENTS'."
– THOMAS L. FRIEDMAN

S. CHWAST

A FEW RICH MEN OWN THE GOVERNMENT
THEY HAVE HOLDINGS IN ARMS MANUFACTURE, BANKING AND OIL
THEY TOOK POWER IN A PHONY ELECTION
THEY WANT TO USE THAT POWER, TO INCREASE THEIR OWN WEALTH
BY SCORING LUCRATIVE DEFENSE CONTRACTS
AND CONTROLING THE WORLD'S SUPPLY OF OIL
THEY WANT TO RULE THE WORLD
9-11 WAS THEIR BIG OPPORTUNITY
IRAQ IS JUST ONE OF A SERIES OF WARS THEY WOULD FIGHT FOR OIL.
WE CAN FOLLOW THEM TO WAR AND DISASTER
OR WE CAN MAKE THIS A REAL DEMOCRACY.

MASTERMIND

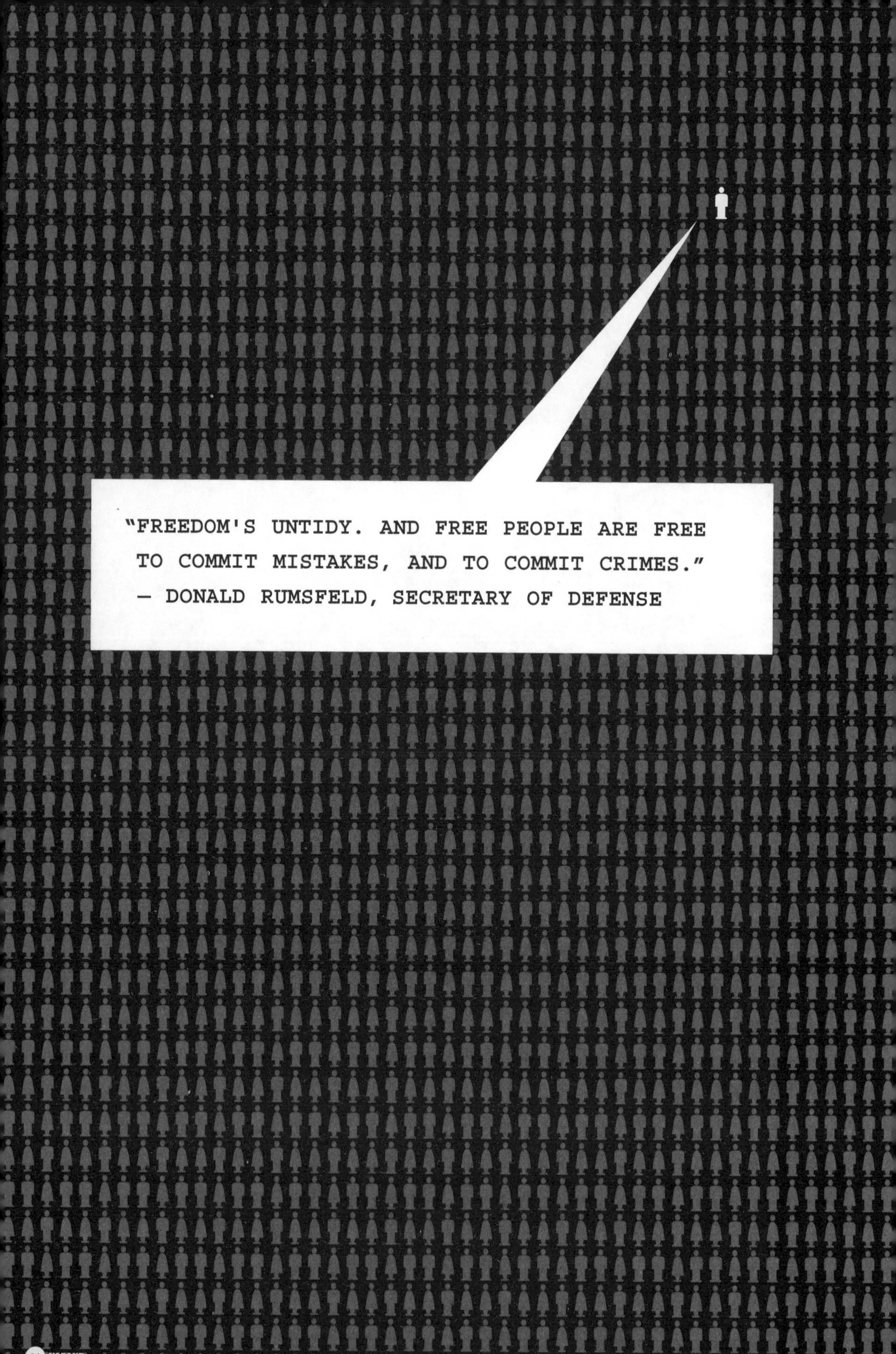
"FREEDOM'S UNTIDY. AND FREE PEOPLE ARE FREE TO COMMIT MISTAKES, AND TO COMMIT CRIMES."
– DONALD RUMSFELD, SECRETARY OF DEFENSE

charles s. anderson design company www.csandersondesign.com

PRY IT FROM MY COLD DEAD FIST
GUNS
21
22
23
24
21 22 23 24 25 24 23 22
24
23
22
21
The republic is defended in 3 stages
1 BALLOT BOX
2 JURY BOX
3 CARTRIDGE BOX
-Eric Schaub
AMERICA
GUN CONTROL
THE BEST DEFENSE AGAINST IMPERIALISM IS A WELL ARMED POPULOUS

EMBRACE ETHNIC FOOD DIVERSITY
GLOBE
KING'S
Food Host
A
FREE
Taco
Repu
Kentucky
DISCOVER AM
MAIL ME NOW MAI
Empire
mart
Empire
el taco
FREE
NOW MAIL ME NOW MAIL
Empire
Mista
DONU
MORE
AMERICA
CULTURAL CROCKPOT
TRADEMARKING THE WORLD'S CULTURES AND SELLING THEM BACK

CASUAL FRIDAY IN MANHATTAN
Countries that possess a demonstrated capability and willingness to use chem-bio weapons, and who develop far more nasty forms of biological-terror weapons, are a threat not just to us but to the global survival of all mankind. Iraq, from all the evidence available, including recent defectors, is the world's leading threat. — Stephen Bryen
ARE WE NEXT
AMERICA
CHEM-BIO WEAPONS
SADDAM HUSSEIN HAS USED CHEMICAL WEAPONS ON HIS OWN PEOPLE

Be not intimidated ... nor suffer yourselves to be wheeled out of your liberties by any pretense of politeness, delicacy, or decency. These, as they are often used, are but three different names for hypocrisy, chicanery, and cowardice.
— John Adams

AMERICA

TOUGH LOVE

HE WHO WANTS PEACE MUST PREPARE FOR WAR —Claudius

CLOUDED VISION
WAR IS WRONG
SO ARE OPRESSIVE, MURDEROUS DICTATORS WHO PRODUCE NUCLEAR, BIOLOGICAL, AND CHEMICAL WEAPONS
AMERICA
EMPIRE BY DEFAULT?
ETERNAL VIGILANCE IS THE PRICE OF LIBERTY—Wendel Phillips

THIS CAN'T MISS
BY ROBERT GROSSMAN
Now we've got it! A way to find Saddam or Bin Laden or anyone else we're looking for.
It's called H2HSEP!
Wow!
Leave it to good old American ingenuity! Is it some kind of new evil-doer-seeking molecule?
No.
Is it a giant vacuum cleaner that sucks people out of bunkers!
Uh-uh.
How about a million heavily armed, highly intelligent, indestructible robots that can also fly and go underwater?
Not exactly.
So what does H2HSEP stand for?
House To House Search of the Entire Planet!
Solid!

Attention (natural) citizens:

Don't be mistaken for an evil doer!

Support the National I.D. Program

· AMERICAN SAMOA · SPA… …RGIN ISLANDS · UNITED KIN…

JOIN THE TRIBUTE TO FREEDOM TEAM!

DoD™

AMERICA'S OLDEST, LARGEST, BUSIEST, AND MOST SUCCESSFUL COMPANY

We are the world's largest company, with locations in 146 countries, over 2 million employees, and 600,000+ buildings and structures on more than 30 million acres of land. We specialize in warfighting, peace-keeping, humanitarian efforts, evacuation, and homeland security.

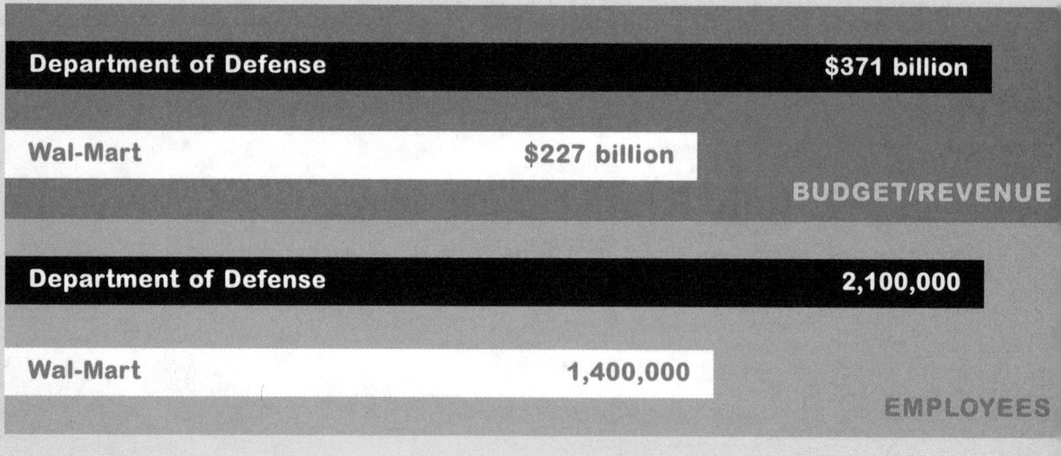

Did you know? The Department of Defense (DoD) has existed since 1949 and employs more people than the next four largest companies (Wal-Mart, Exxon/Mobil, GM, and Ford) in the United States combined. It also has a larger budget/revenue than any two of these put together.

HAITI · SINGAPORE · AFGHANISTAN · SOUTH KOREA · OMAN · MARSHALL ISLA… …DA · NORWAY ·

…CE · HONDURAS · COLUMBIA · ICELAND · BAHRAIN · JAPAN · PORTUGAL ·

NEW ZEALAND · KWAJALEIN ATOLL · BAHAMAS ISLANDS · ITALY · GUAM ·

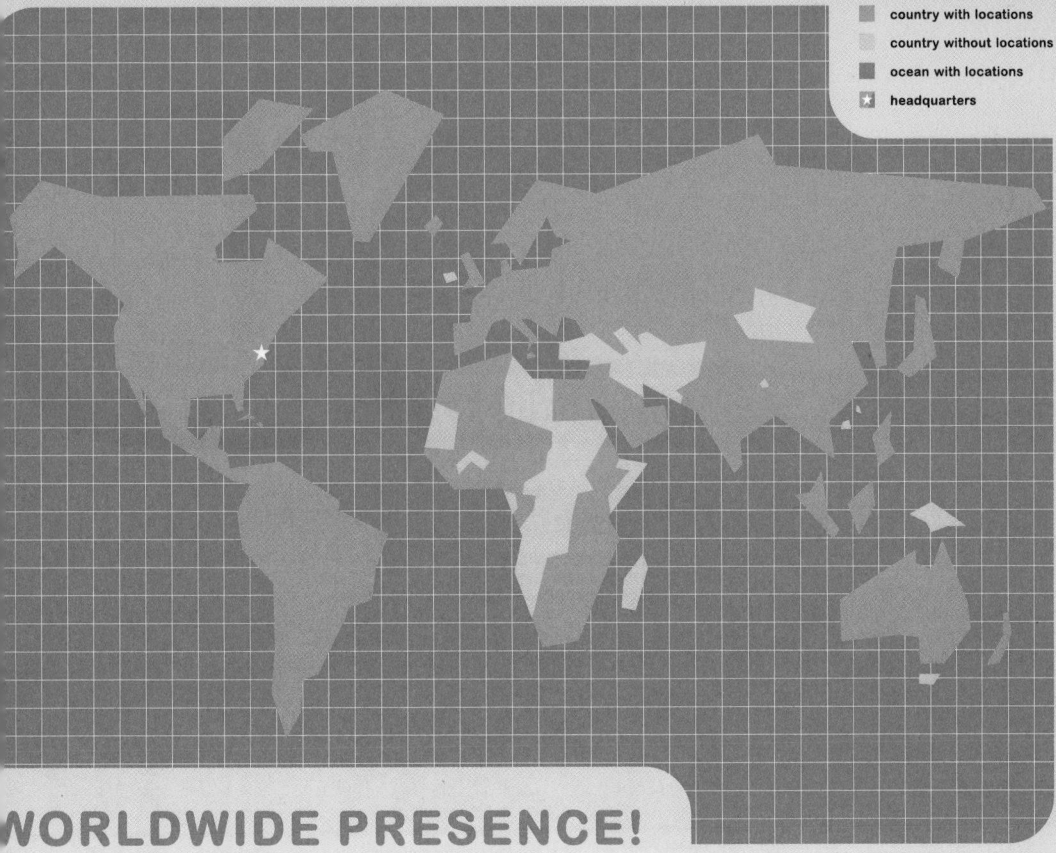

WORLDWIDE PRESENCE!

**"We will help you.
We are here to help you."
— Donald Rumsfeld**

)oD is currently undergoing a transformation.
ransformation is the process whereby DoD is over-auling the establishment to enable it to counter he 21st century most effectively. Transformation is bout new ways of thinking, and organizing the DoD nd its operations—as well as about acquiring new ystem capabilities. To increase effectiveness, he Department is advancing new operational oncepts, and organizational changes, as well as xpanded joint experimentation and training.

ALL TEXT AND FIGURES TAKEN FROM THE DEPARTMENT OF DEFENSE WEBSITE AT HTTP://WWW.DEFENSELINK.MIL/PUBS/DOD101/DOD101FOR2002/DOD101FOR2002_FILES/FRAME.HTM

WAKE ISLAND · GREENLAND · AUSTRALIA · COLUMBIA · INDONESIA · BELGIUM · KENYA · DENMARK ·

LUXEMBOURG · EGYPT · INDIA · GERMANY · NETHERLANDS · VIETNAM ·

THIS IS THE MODERN WORLD

THE FUTURE
OF TECHNOLOGY...
IS A CONTRADICTION IN TERMS.

MARTHA STEWART
Lying
TSK! TSK! MARTHA!
If a man's home is his castle, Martha Stewart's home is her empire. With an all-American combination of will, talent, and consumerist relentlessness, she's made herself the home design dominatrix of middle-class decoration, embodying the "getting over the Joneses" jones of the faux nouveau riche. Martha is omnipresent. Her company, Martha Stuart Living Omnimedia, is self-explanatory.

"HASSLED BY THE MAN"

COLLECTABLE CORPORATE STICKERS

After years of being mentally and financially bitch-slapped by the likes of WorldCom, Enron and Tyco, there's bound to be a "Hassled By The Man" sticker that's right for you. Use them on envelopes when paying bills, writing letters to the editor, or handing over your resignation. Sticky backing makes them easily slappable onto the greasiest, slimiest corporate forehead.

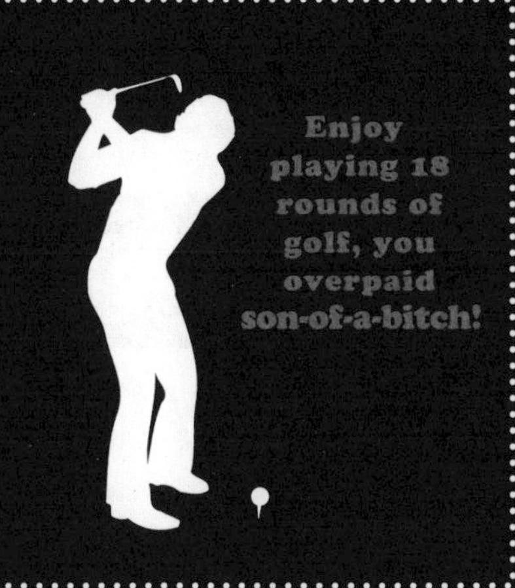
Enjoy playing 18 rounds of golf, you overpaid son-of-a-bitch!

You

Thank-you for your business.

Investments may vary due to market fluctuations.

Please take a look at our grievance policy.

No ... really, let me be the fall guy, for your ineptness at work.

What? I feel fine.

Thanks for the raise.

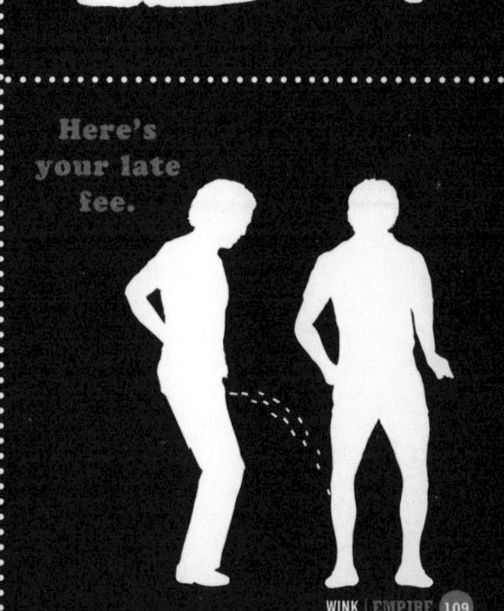
Here's your late fee.

KEVIN BACON LINKED TO OSAMA BIN LADEN

KEVIN BACON

EDDIE ALBERT

RONALD REAGAN

GEORGE BUSH, SR.

GEORGE W. BUSH, JR.

OSAMA BIN LADEN

[KEVIN BACON performed in the 1989 movie *The Big Picture*. One of his costars was veteran actor EDDIE ALBERT.]

[EDDIE ALBERT was in the 1961 motion picture *The Young Doctors*, a film that was narrated by RONALD REAGAN.]

[RONALD REAGAN was President of the U.S.A. from 1983–1989. For both terms, his VeePee was GEORGE BUSH, SR.]

[GEORGE BUSH, SR. was elected President from 1989–92. He is the father of President GEORGE W. BUSH, JR.]

[GEORGE W. BUSH, JR.'s oil companies were funded by rich Saudis and the family of OSAMA BIN LADEN.]

Simple Items

SEE and SAY

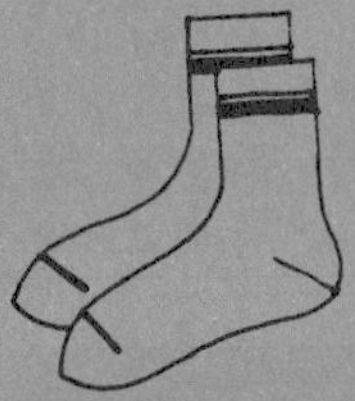
Socks

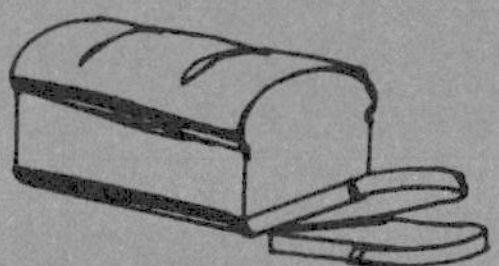
Bread

Dress

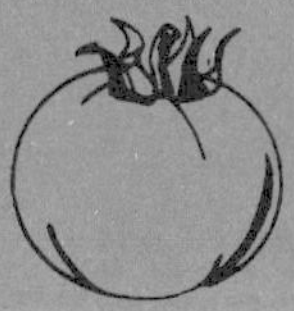
Tomato

Evil Doer

Bowl

Anthrax

Shirt

Bomb

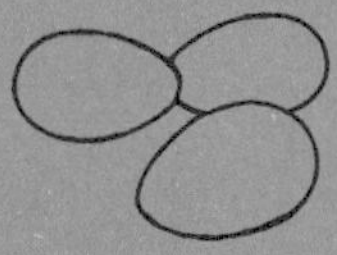
Eggs

Terrorism

Shoes

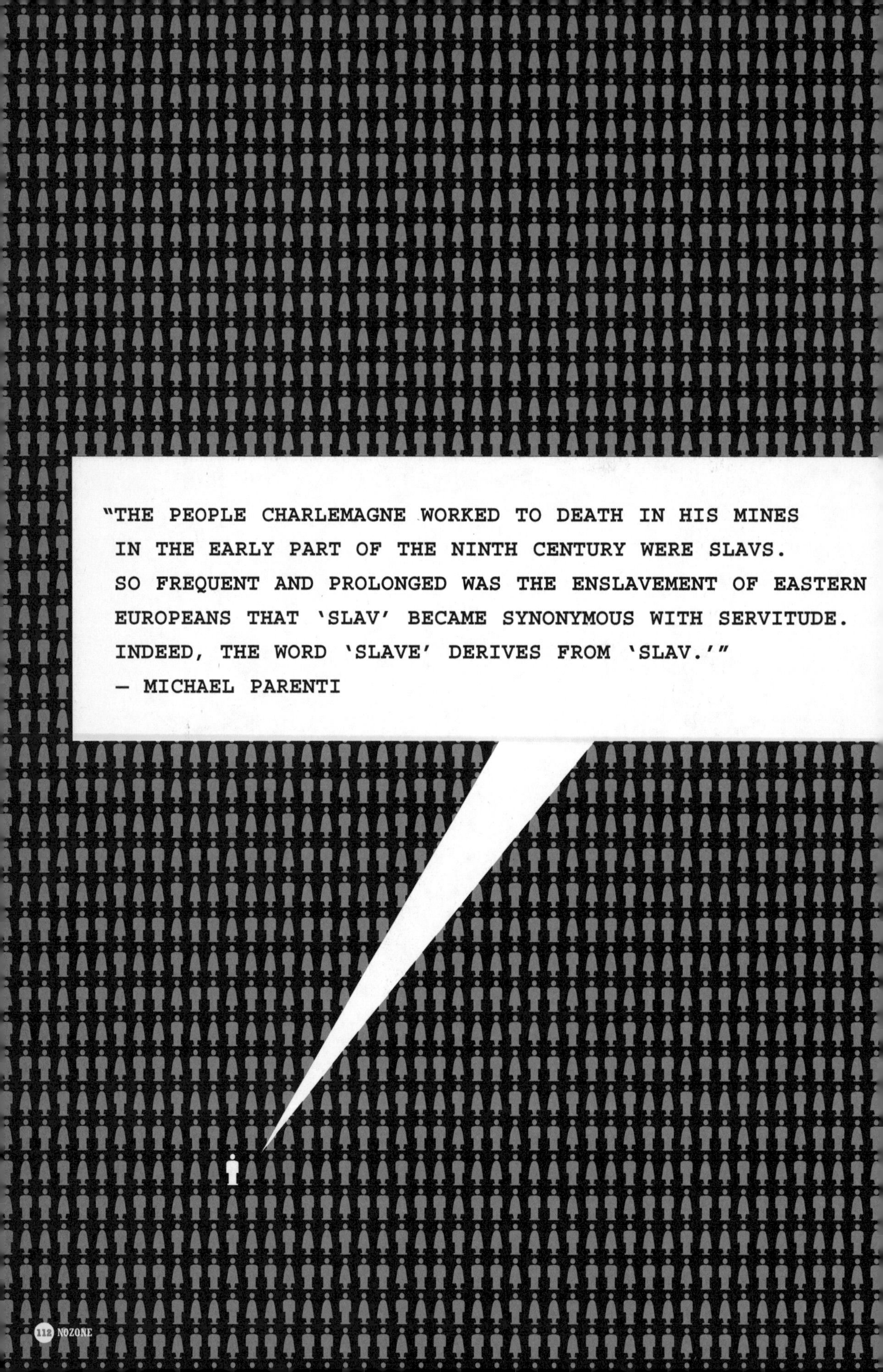
"THE PEOPLE CHARLEMAGNE WORKED TO DEATH IN HIS MINES IN THE EARLY PART OF THE NINTH CENTURY WERE SLAVS. SO FREQUENT AND PROLONGED WAS THE ENSLAVEMENT OF EASTERN EUROPEANS THAT 'SLAV' BECAME SYNONYMOUS WITH SERVITUDE. INDEED, THE WORD 'SLAVE' DERIVES FROM 'SLAV.'"
— MICHAEL PARENTI

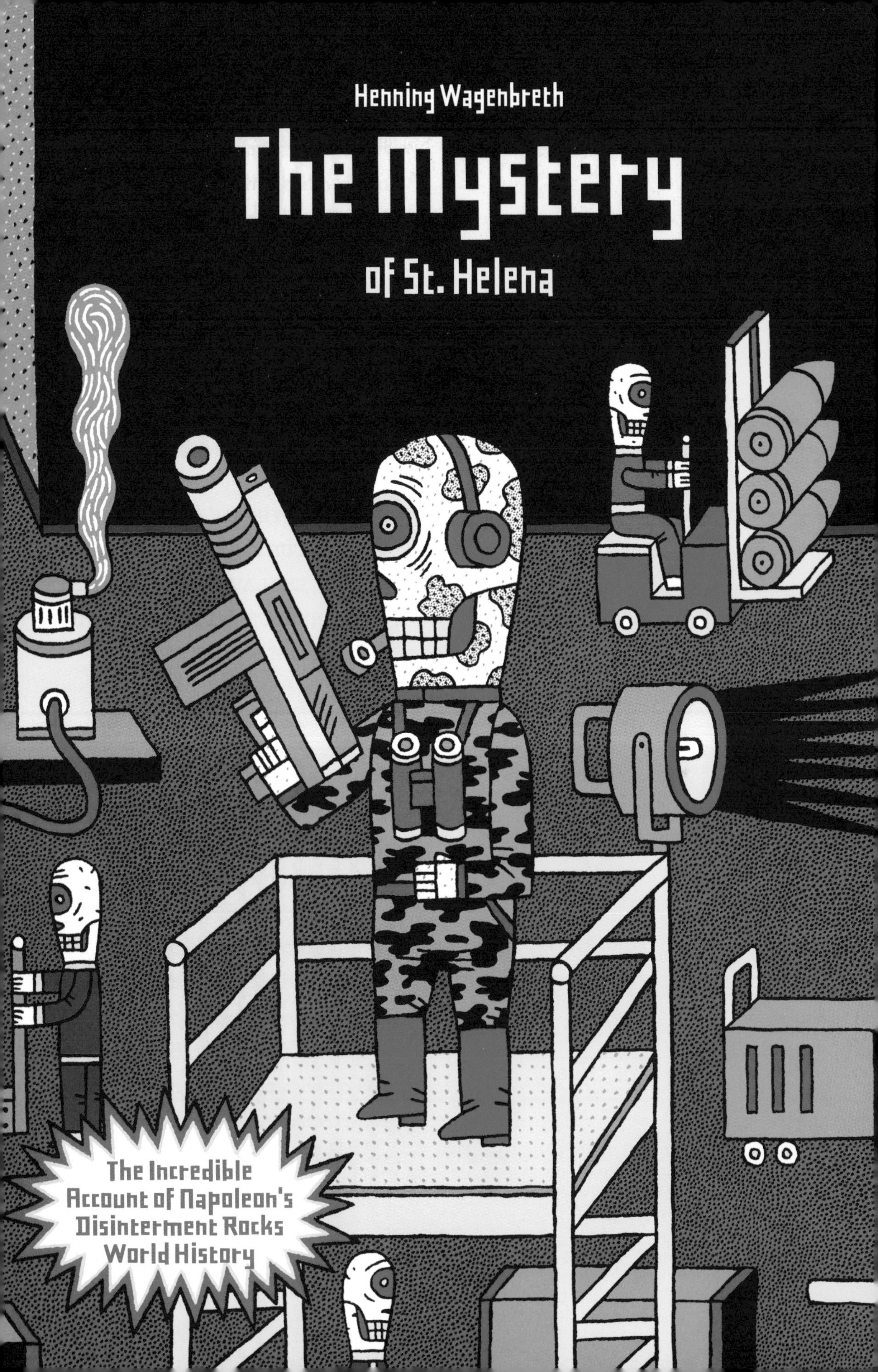
Henning Wagenbreth
The Mystery
of St. Helena
The Incredible
Account of Napoleon's
Disinterment Rocks
World History

"Today the Emperor remarked that his sorely criticized bulletins had always been faithful to the truth, the only exception being the deviations necessitated by the proximity of the enemy."

Napoleon died in 1821 in the company of his closest followers and in the presence of the English governor. He was buried on the island of St. Helena.

Nineteen years later:

My encounter with Napoleon in the grave on St. Helena.

The Journal of Count de Rohan-Chabot

"The closer one gets to the island, the more frightful the sight of it. Jamestown Valley resembles the entrance to hell."
General Montholon,
Napoleon's companion in exile

Upon the order of the French government, I proceeded to St. Helena aboard the frigate "La Belle-Poule," accompanied by the physician Dr. Guillard, in order to disinter the mortal remains of Napoleon. After sailing across the Atlantic for eight weeks, we arrived at the island and disembarked on October 14, 1840. The wind was whistling across the bleak cliffs. It was cold and unpleasant. Passing clouds kept hiding the moon. We reached the grave at the stroke of midnight. Dust would probably be all that remained of him who lay therein, whose name and power once struck the world with awe.

Expedition Route

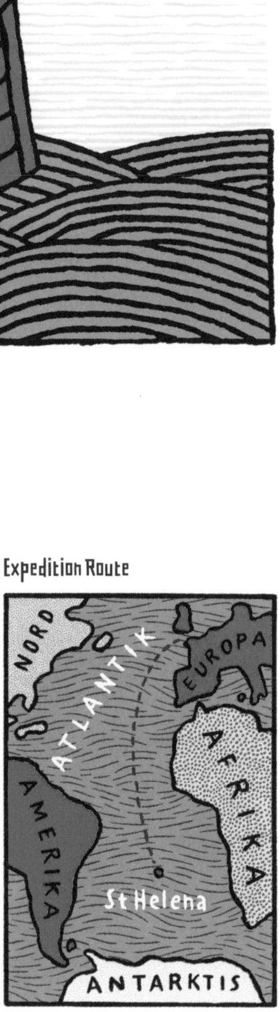

Night

The burial slab consisted of such hard material that it could only be removed using hammer and chisel. We climbed down and found the coffin in good condition.

Vault

At my behest, Dr. Guillard proceeded to open the coffin. The lid came away at once and to our astonishment we found only a pillow and a few worms inside.

Bunker

Troubled by the failure to find his Majesty's body, we examined the vault with great care and discovered a passage leading to additional subterranean chambers.

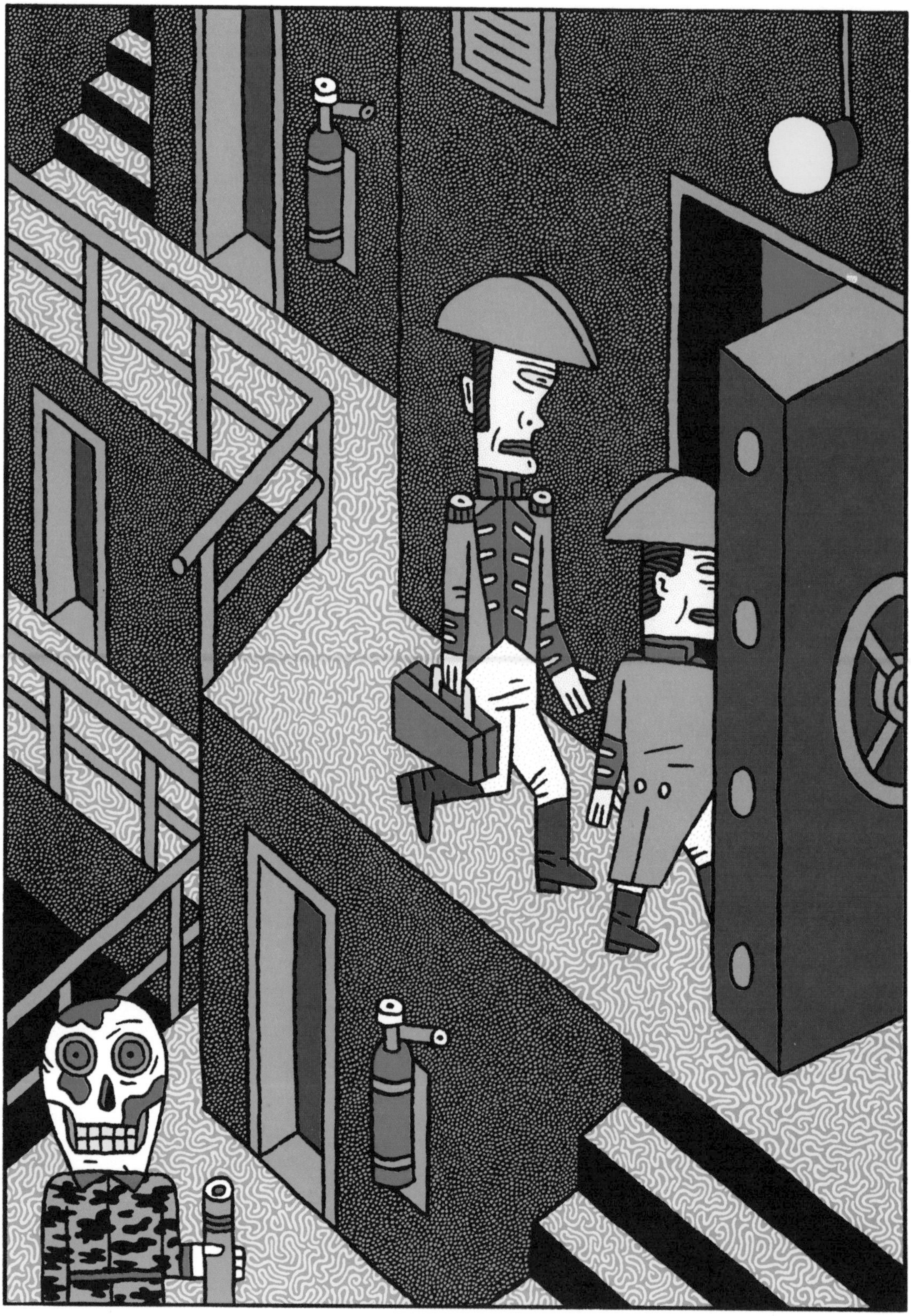

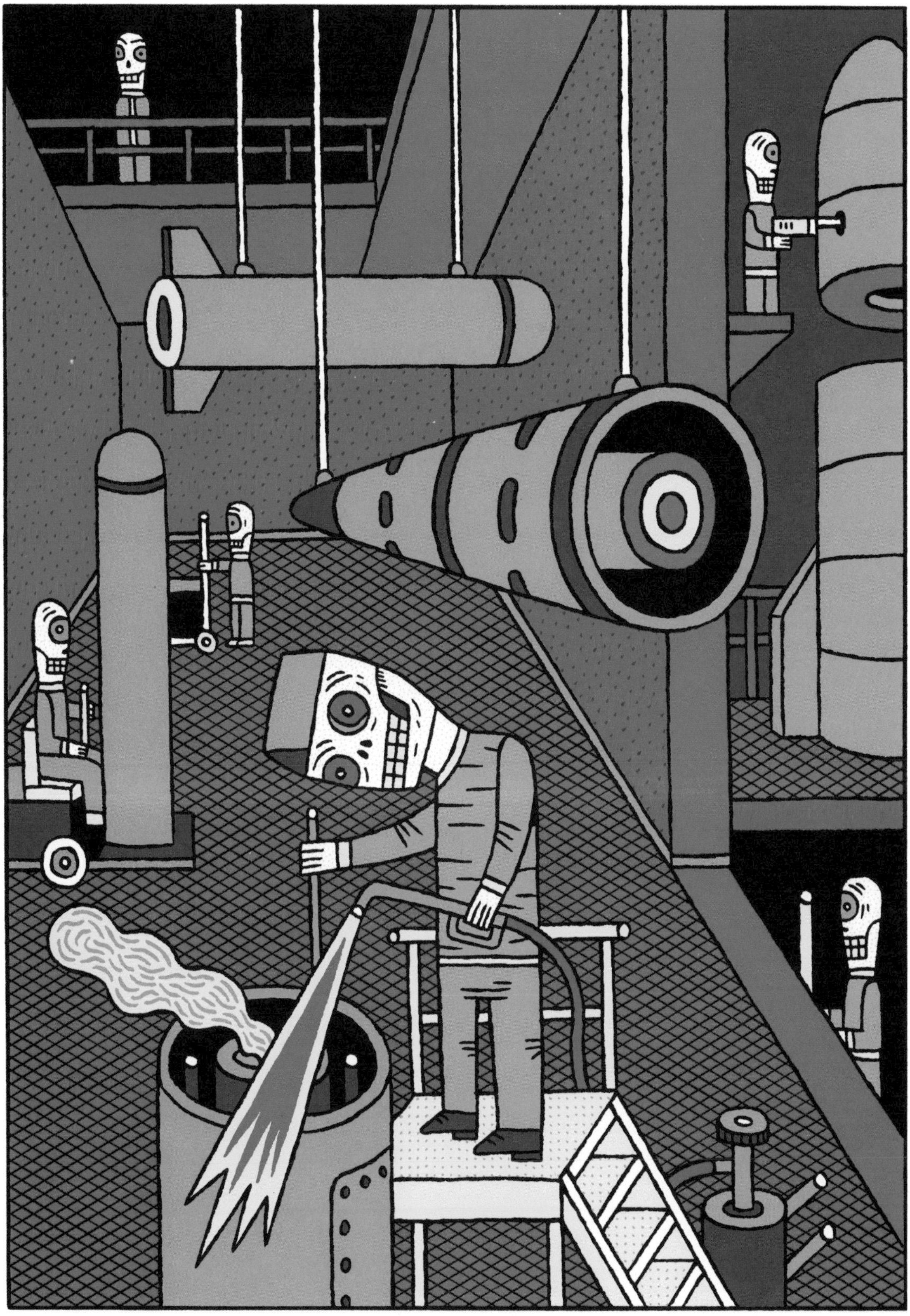

The blows of heavy hammers and the rumble of engines echoed in a tunnel. We came upon furious activity amid spraying sparks and wafting smoke.

Factory

South Atlantic Station

This could only be the work of the devil or Napoleon. Such dynamics and precision! The air seemed permeated with the visionary spirit of the Emperor, with his will and unbridled energy.

City

We had undoubtedly come upon an advanced civilization. Our curiosity made us careless. We were discovered by security guards and taken to the High Command.

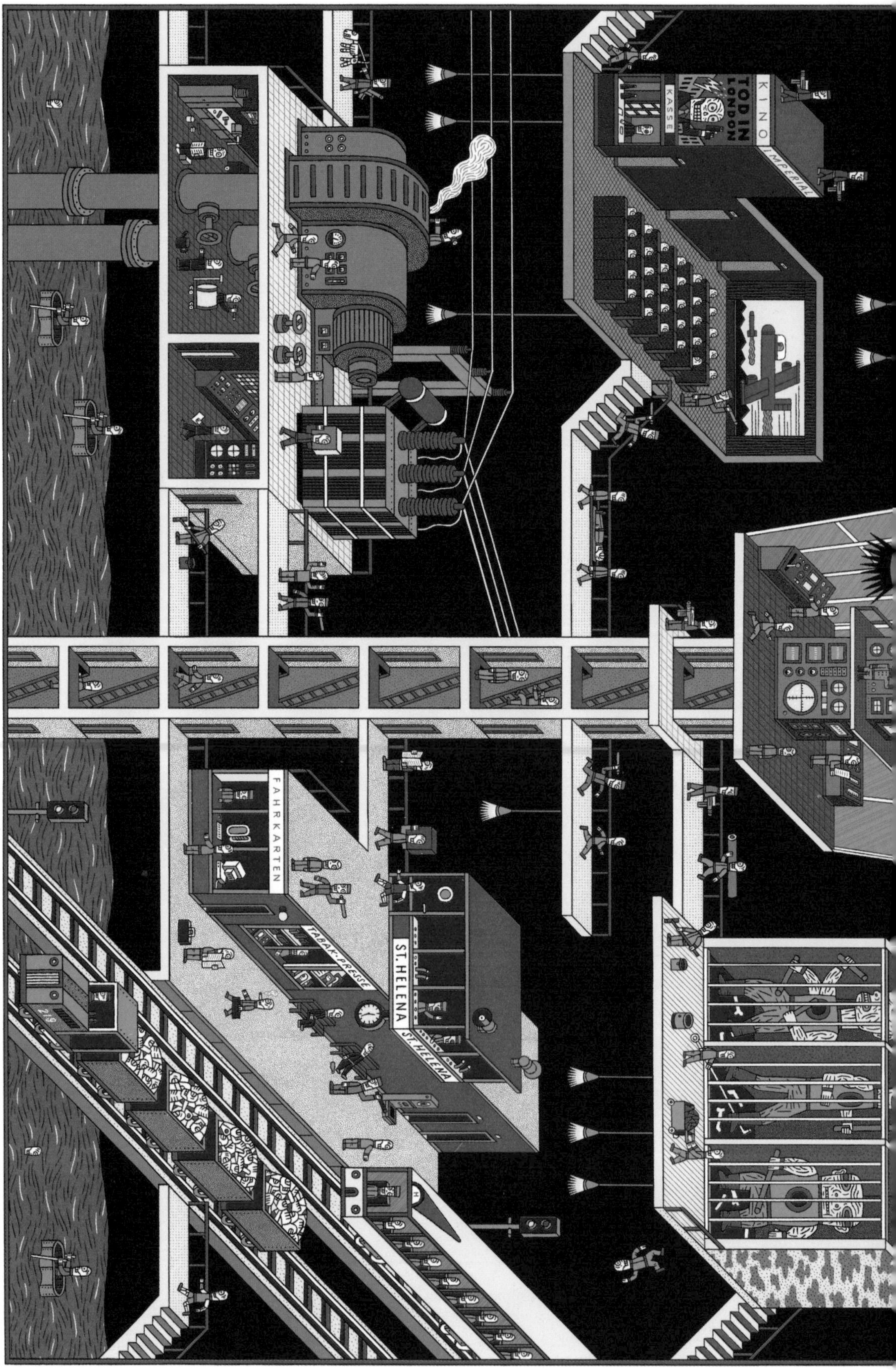
KINO
IMPERIAL
TOD IN LONDON
KASSE
FAHRKARTEN
TABAK-PRESSE
ST. HELENA
ST. HELENA

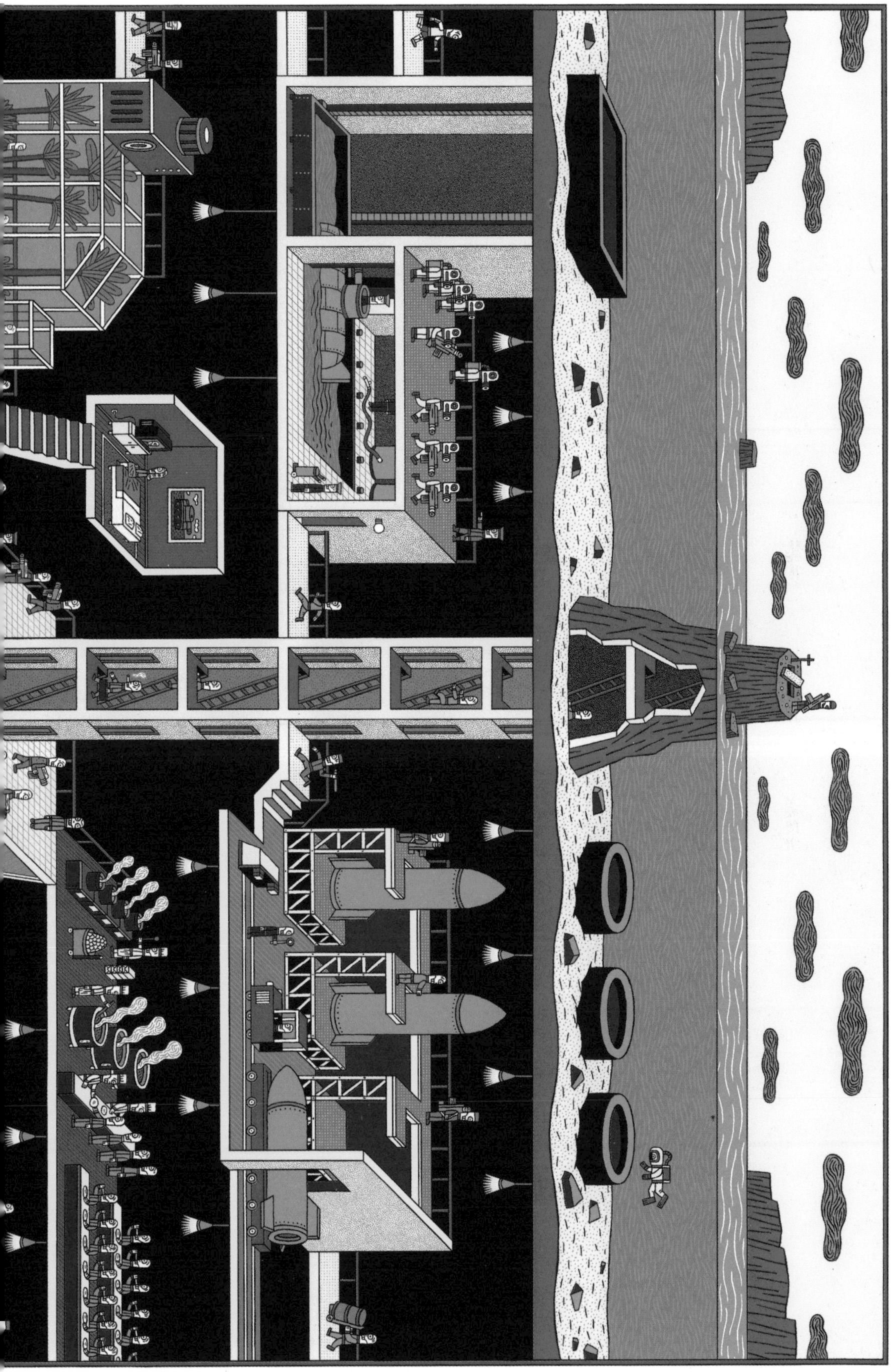

High Command

I recognized Napoleon at once. Not only was he well preserved but his face still retained its authentic expression. The Emperor extolled the efficiency of his government:

"Every nod is instantly communicated to millions – an absolute necessity if I wish to conquer the immeasurable difficulties that have confronted me from the outset."

Central Registry

Waterloo
Plant

"Millions of soldiers fell in my wars. All the freedom I can grant these utterly ignorant masses, demoralized by anarchy and war, shall be granted."

"Nature has created all men equal. I feel called upon to give free rein to all the gifted, regardless of birth or fortune."

Processing Plant

Sports

"Here I devote undivided attention to physical training for it instills discipline, fosters a team spirit, and increases mental performance."

"Great deeds can be achieved only by obeying the natural rules of war. One must treat war scientifically and possess the secret of turning one's armies into veritable machines."

B1

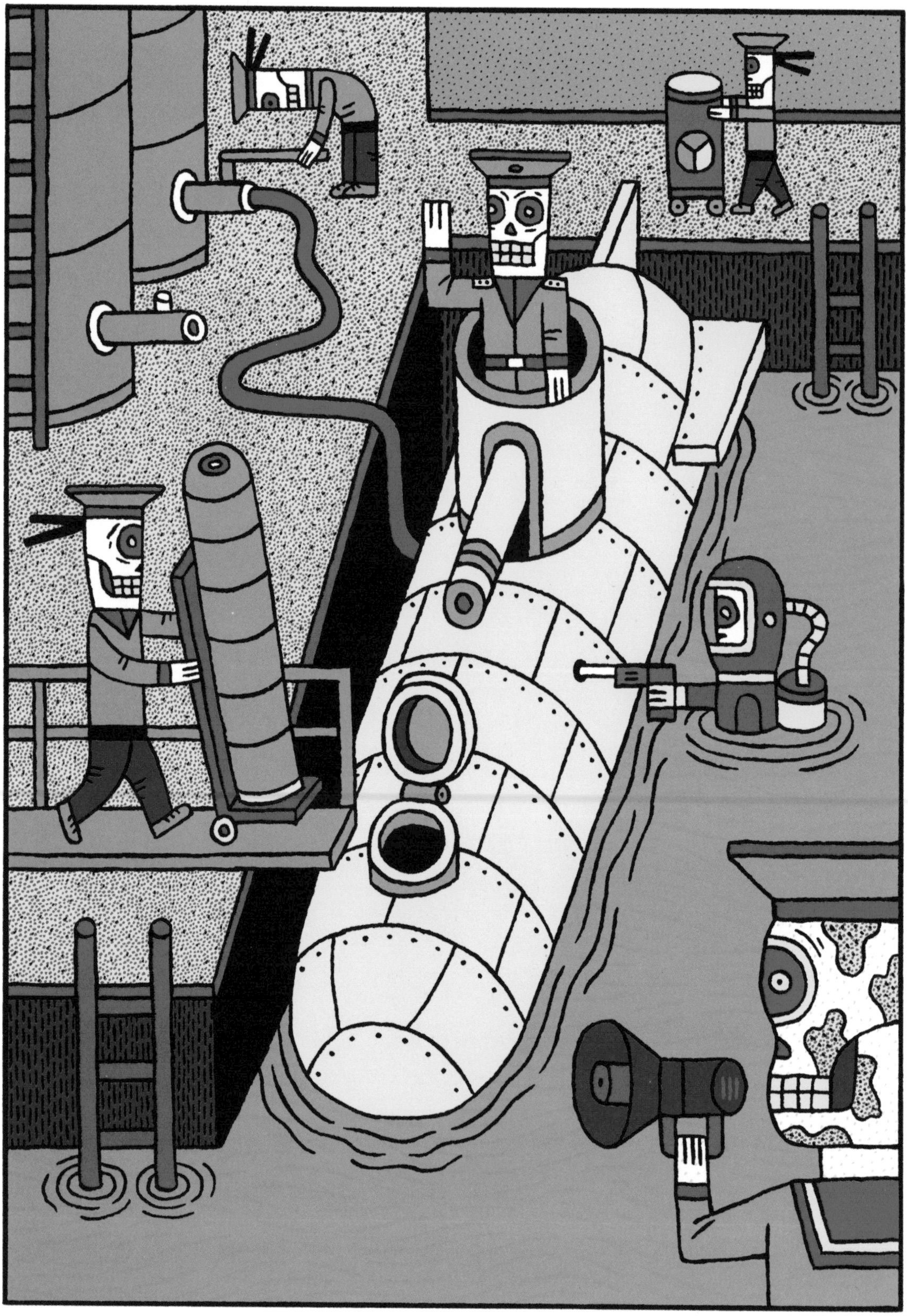

Politics

"I have never made a conquest unless it was essential to my defense. Europe relentlessly opposed my political principles. One must defeat so as not to be defeated. The threat is always

the same, the battle horrendous, and the crisis menacingly nigh. A young state must necessarily be unyielding. In more tranquil times, I shall implement the transition to a constitutional government."

LABORATORY 49

For the artificial breeding of agents and saboteurs

"Spies must be well treated to prevent them from defecting. If they are not richly rewarded and do not enjoy great confidence, this is tantamount to political suicide."

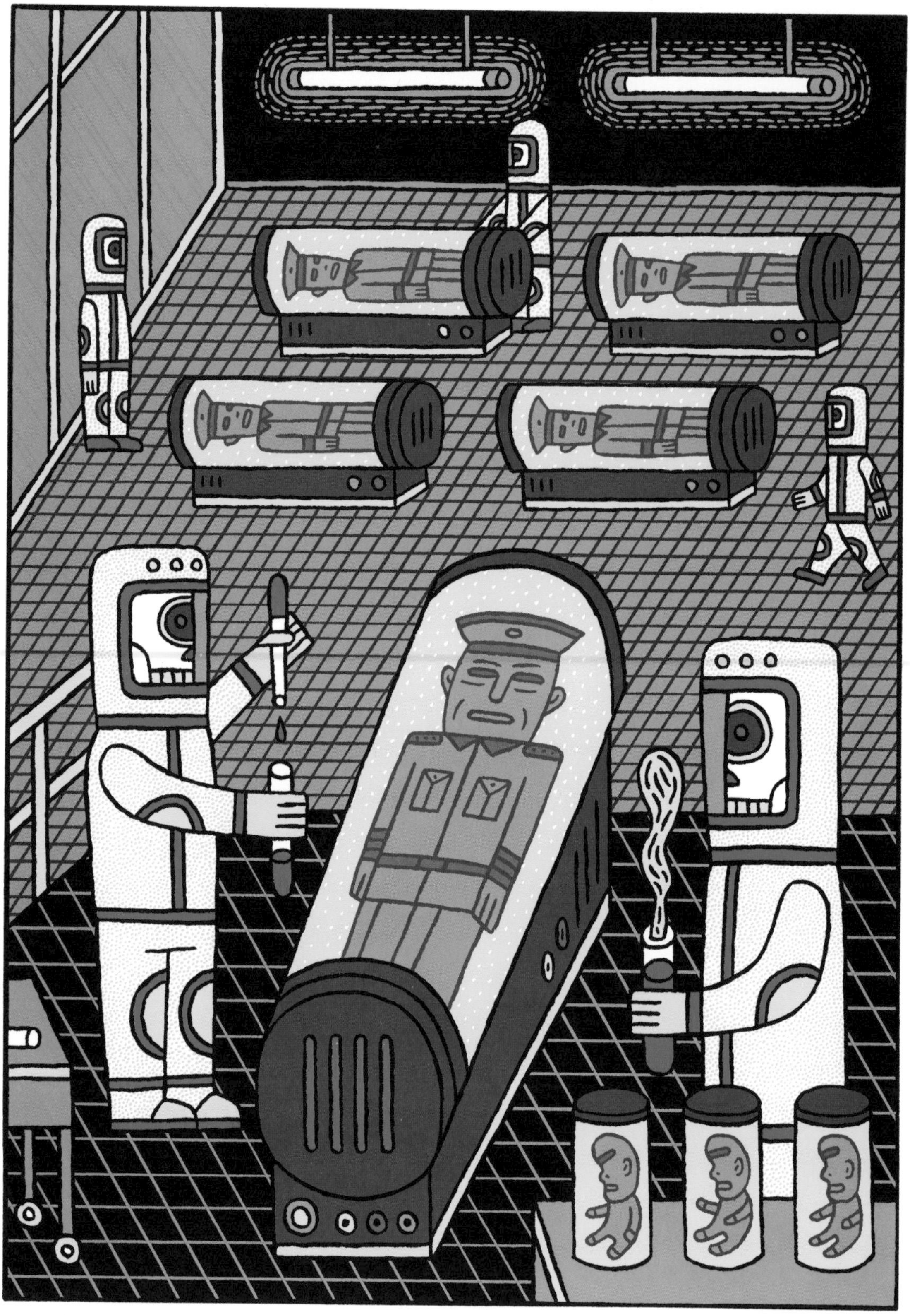

"The use of physical violence does not exclude intelligence. Victory is the prerogative of the ruthless. Mistakes caused by kindness are the worst."

Gas

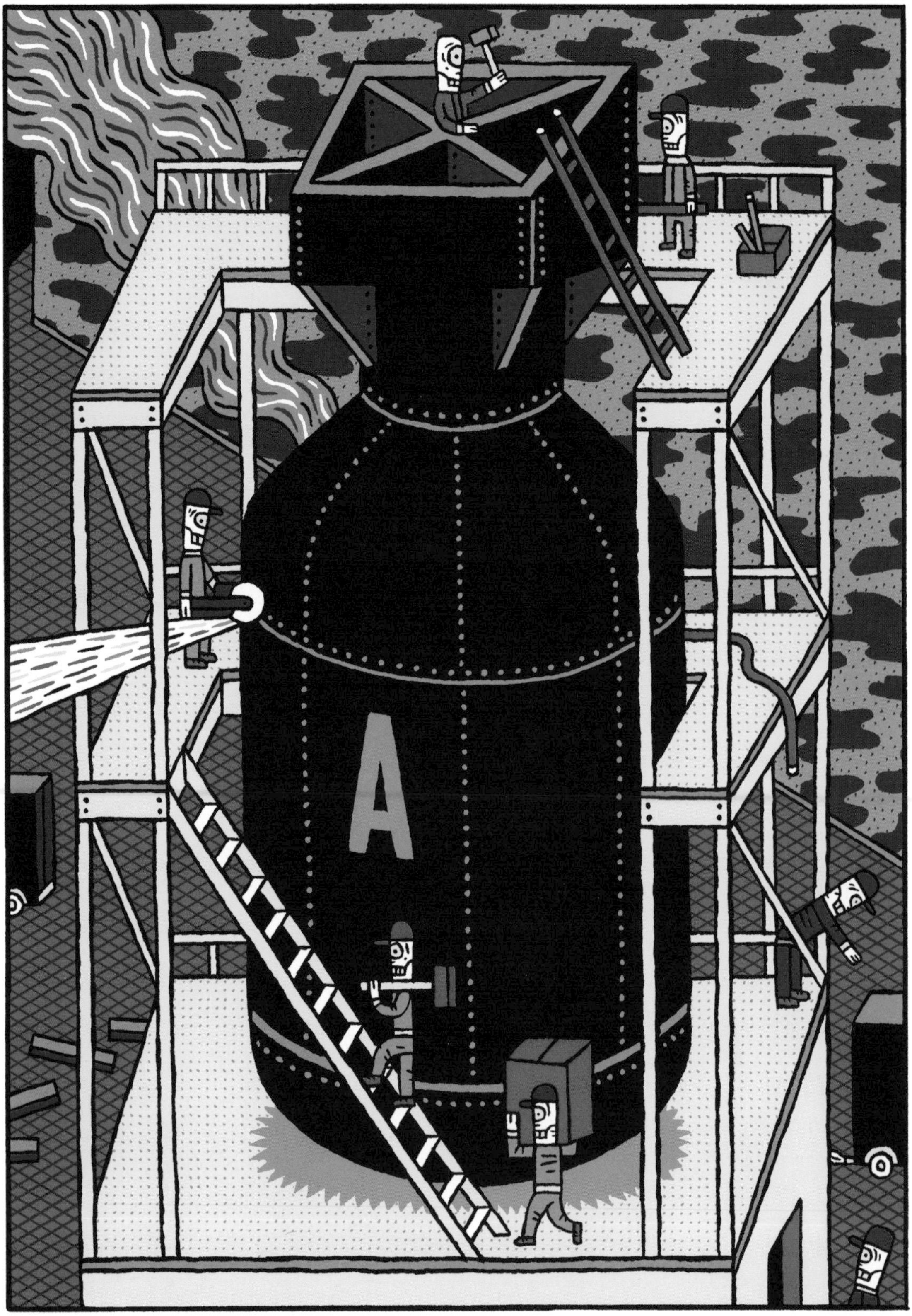

"Three more years and I shall be the master of the universe. I shall be vindicated. The truth will come to light and the errors will be weighed against the good I have done. I admit, my ambition is great."

When the Emperor had concluded his strategic remarks, I read out the order of the French government: "Napoleon's remains are to be transported to Paris for formal burial."

Alarm

at the High Command

Escape

Napoleon disagreed violently: he had no desire to molder in a coffin as a national monument. We then met with severe hostility from which we were compelled to withdraw in great haste.

THE END

THE GREAT VILLAINS OF WORLD HISTORY

Throughout the course of world history, individuals with an insatiable hunger for power, a grandiose charisma, and a desire for immortality have terrorized millions, caused war and genocide, and inspired a vast array of literature. In the last century, film and television have contributed a new variety of villains to the fray. Today, when we think of the greatest villains of the world, as many have been real as imagined. The list compiled herein does not discriminate between mythical and tangible villains, nor does it give preference to those with more air time on the cultural radar. While this inventory of great villains is not intended to be comprehensive, we think it illustrates the breadth of our contemporary imagination for conceiving of villainy.

Voivode Dracolya (a.k.a. Vlad the Impaler)
approx. 1431–85 A.D.
Despotic Murderous Ruler
Romania

Vlad the Impaler ruled Wallachia, part of what is now Romania, during the Ottoman Empire's attempts to conquer parts of Europe in the fifteenth century. During one of these invasions, a young Vlad was taken captive by the Turkish Sultan and imprisoned in Istanbul, a trauma that scholars have speculated may have been the germination for his sadistic tendencies. After seven years in captivity Vlad escaped and returned to his homeland, beginning his gory reign. Vlad routinely pillaged small towns in his territory, slaughtering hundreds of peasants. As suggested by his nickname, his favored means of execution was impalement. According to legend, Vlad would drive his victims in herds over cliffs onto beds of spikes below. On one occasion one of Vlad's mistresses, who lied by saying she was carrying a child, was gutted from her pubic area to her breasts so that, Vlad remarked, he could, "Let the world see where I have been." No one was spared from Vlad's gory vengeance. On another occasion he invited the "old, the ill, the lame, the poor, the blind, and the vagabonds" of his country to a feast in his castle, only to incinerate all of his helpless guests after the meal. During his brief six-year rule Vlad is estimated to have murdered between 40,000 and 100,000 people. Vlad inspired a vast written and pictorial legacy during his life, which coincided with the invention of the printing press. He was also the basis for the character of Dracula in Bram Stoker's 1897 novel of the same name. Stoker's creation became a touchstone for the nineteenth century Gothic school of literature and was the basis for dozens of movies and innumerable books. As a contemporary movement, Goth has found sympathy with many serial killers and sociopaths.

Saloth Sar (a.k.a. Pol Pot)
1925–98
Genocidal Communist Leader
Cambodia

Saloth Sar was a Cambodian tyrant who was born to a prosperous family living comfortably under the king's protection. After studying Marxism in Paris in the 1950s, Saloth Sar chose Pol Pot as his nom de guerre. He returned to Cambodia and began organizing communist revolts, finally overthrowing the government in 1975. Pol Pot's Cambodian "Democratic Kampuchea" regime declared "Year Zero" and began a radical program to create an idealized communist, xenophobic society, commencing one of the largest genocides of the twentieth century. Pot oversaw the death of 1.5 million Cambodians from malnutrition and illness after forced internment in government-run work camps. He also ordered the systematic torture and execution of another 200,000 Cambodians, targeting intellectuals, landowners, and other groups and individuals whom he perceived as a threat to his zealous vision. Notably, Pot's army photographed and cataloged all of his victims before murdering them. The Cambodian government still has thousands of these photographs of victims, each holding an ominous number.

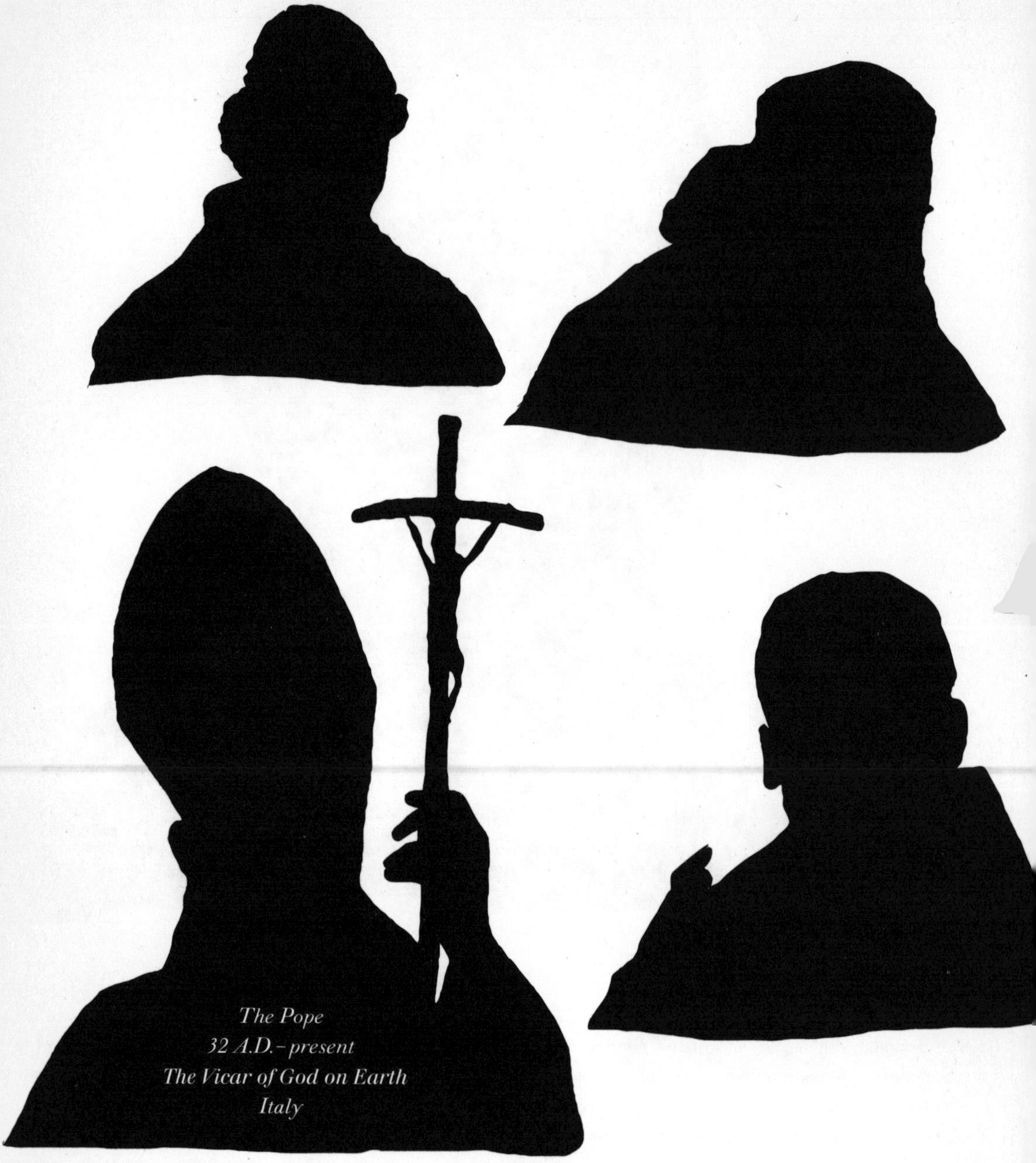

The Pope
32 A.D.–present
The Vicar of God on Earth
Italy

Although the Pope has been worshipped for thousands of years as the vicar of God on Earth, since the first Pope, St. Paul, was anointed by Jesus Christ in 32 A.D. to the present, the papacy has been plagued by thousands of years of corruption. Its crimes have included bribery, war, ethnic and religious cleansing, rape, and torture. Some of the most notorious popes include Pope John XII, who turned the Lateran Palace into a brothel, and Pope Alexander VI, who on one occasion commanded fifty prostitutes to engage in sexual acts for his entertainment. Between the eleventh and fourteenth centuries, the pope ordered the Crusades, a series of military expeditions to wrest Jerusalem and other parts of the Holy Land from Muslim control. Beginning with the Peasants Crusade and the Slaughter of Innocents, the nine Crusades included the disasterous Children's Crusade, in which thousands of children were killed to the rallying words, "Dieu Le Volt" (God wills it).

The death total for the crusades is estimated at 100,000. Between the fourteenth and nineteenth centuries the papacy oversaw the Inquisition, a program of systematized torture intended to eliminate heretics by torturing suspects and then killing them. More than a million people were tortured and then burned or hanged in the Inquisitions. Because church law forbade the killing, the Inquistitors were notorious for making use of devices such as the "strappado" or pully, and the "aselli" or water torment, which caused intense pain but usually did not cause bleeding. Recently the papal institution has again been blighted, as tens of thousands of children have claimed they were abused by pedophile priests, whose exploitation of children was allegedly concealed and abetted by the Church with the consent of the Pope.

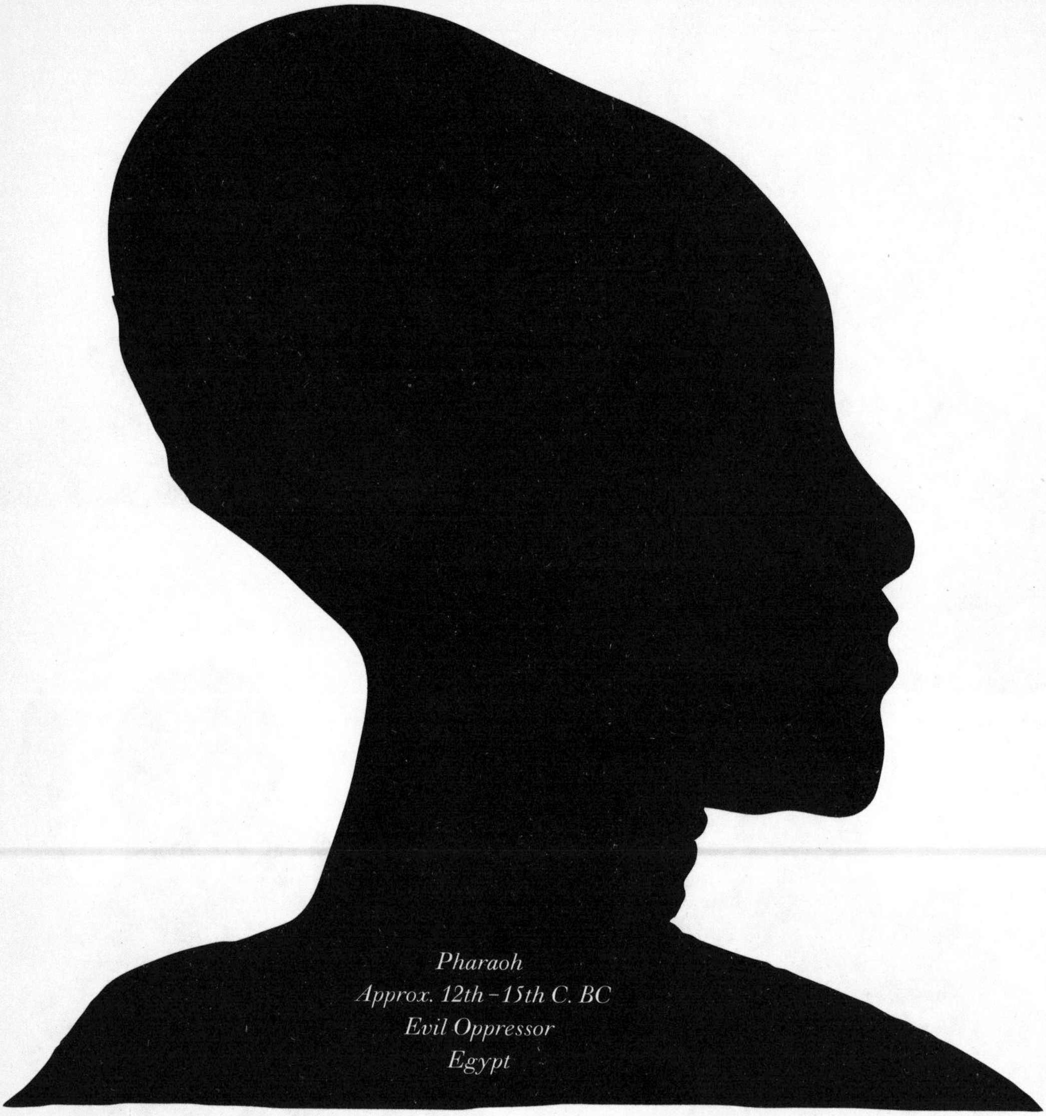

Pharaoh, probably the most iniquitous villain in recorded history, first appears in the Book of Genesis in the Old Testament. According to biblical legend, Jacob and his tribe members fled a famine in Palestine and migrated south to Egypt. They were greeted in their new land by the evil Egyptian king, known in the Bible only as "Pharaoh," who was furious that his new contingency would threaten his rule and ordered their enslavement. For hundreds of years, Pharaoh, whom scholars have speculated was based on Ramses II, ruled mercilessly over the Israelites, forcing them into bondage and later ordering the drowning of all baby boys. During this time, Moses was born to Israelite parents, who wrapped and floated him in a river to save him from certain death. He was found by Pharaoh's daughter and raised as his son in the royal palace, until he was chosen by God in a vision to free the Israelites from Pharaoh. With the help of ten plagues, Moses liberated the Israelites and led them through the Red Sea out of Egypt, eventually killing Pharoah when the waters again flooded the sea basin. The flight from the villainous Pharaoh is the inspiration for the Jewish Passover celebration, as well as the slave spiritual "Let My People Go." Pharaoh was also immortalized in Cecil B. DeMille's 1956 film *The Ten Commandments*, in which Yul Brynner played the evil ruler.

The Wicked Witch of the West
1939
Despicable Tyrant
The Land of Oz

"I'll get you my pretty, and your little dog, too!" Who could forget this infamous villain's chilling caveat to the innocent Dorothy and dog Toto? The 1939 film *The Wizard of Oz*, based on the L. Frank Baum's fairy tale of the same name, forever changed the color of evil. Before a cyclone whisked Dorothy and her dog out of Kansas to the Land of Oz, a vicious nieghbor named Miss Gulch vows to take Toto "to the sheriff and make sure he's destroyed." When Dorothy was catapulted into Oz, the evil Miss Gulch was reincarnated in the villainous Wicked Witch of the West, whose fury that Dorothy is given the ruby slippers begins in an avalanche of vengeance unleashed at Dorothy and her fellow journeyers. The Wicked Witch, who also tyrannized and enslaved the Winkies and Munchkins, instigated a cruel rampage of crimes against Dorothy and the other pilgrims, including many gruesome attempts at muder by fire, water, poison, and an army of Winkies. She also sent myriad plagues including a pack of forty hungry wolves, a flock of wild crows, a swarm of black bees, and the three creepy flying monkeys to kill Dorothy and her friends, but to no avail. The Wicked Witch met a fate similar to another great villain, Pharaoh, when she died a watery death, melting pathetically when Dorothy threw a bucket of water at her. Scholars have pointed out that the Wicked Witch of the West is based largely on the evil queen embodied as a wicked witch in the Snow White fairy tales, a character who was also called the Evil Queen, and inspired by despotic and narcissistic matriarchs throughout history such as Queen Victoria of England and her imperialist regime.

"BY PURCHASING MONFORT, CONAGRA BECAME THE BIGGEST MEATPACKER IN THE WORLD. TODAY IT IS THE LARGEST FOODSERVICE SUPPLIER IN NORTH AMERICA. IN ADDITION TO BEING THE NUMBER-ONE PRODUCER OF FRENCH FRIES (THROUGH ITS LAMB WESTON SUBSIDIARY), CONAGRA IS ALSO THE NATION'S LARGEST SHEEP AND TURKEY PROCESSOR, THE LARGEST DISTRIBUTOR OF AGRICULTURAL CHEMICALS, THE SECOND-LARGEST MANUFACTURER OF FROZEN FOODS, THE SECOND-LARGEST FLOUR MILLER, THE THIRD-LARGEST CHICKEN AND PORK PROCESSOR, AS WELL AS A LEADING SEED PRODUCER, FEED PRODUCER, AND COMMODITY FUTURES TRADER. THE COMPANY SELLS ITS FOOD UNDER ABOUT ONE HUNDRED CONSUMER BRAND NAMES, INCLUDING HUNT'S, ARMOUR, LA CHOY, COUNTRY PRIDE, SWISS MISS, ORVILLE REDENBACHER'S , REDDI-WIP, TASTE O'SEA, KNOTTS'S BERRY FARM, HEBREW NATIONAL, AND HEALTHY CHOICE. ALTHOUGH FEW AMERICANS HAVE HEARD OF CONAGRA, THEY ARE LIKELY TO EAT AT LEAST ONE OF ITS PRODUCTS EVERY DAY."

– ERIC SCHLOSSER

Our Daily Bread

R.O. Blechman

The Abbey of St. Crispus (Apologia, N.Y. 12534) was renowned for its bread.

It was baked using a 125-year-old oven and a 260-year-old-formula.

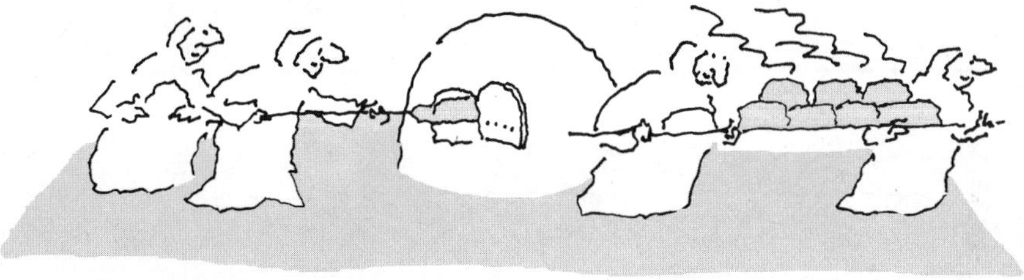

The bread was delivered in a 74-year-old station wagon.

It sometimes broke down.

The fame of *Our Daily Bread* spread throughout the Northeast.

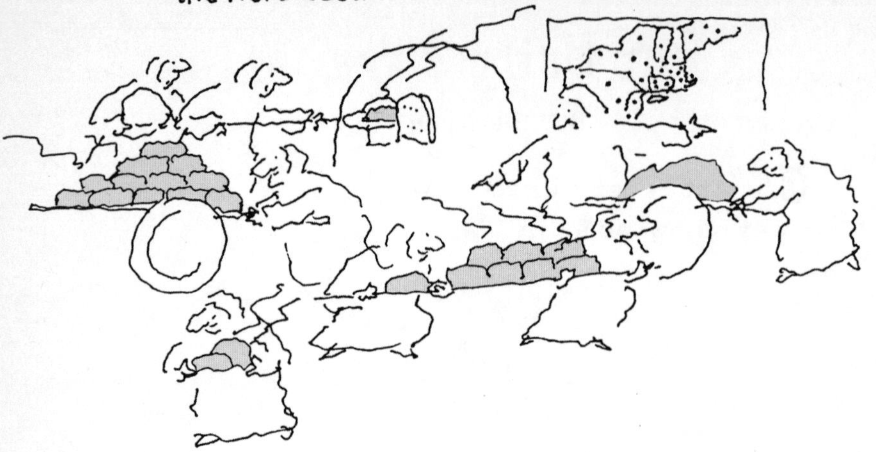

Word of its success soon reached the corporate headquarters of Krassko Kookery.

Nutrition experts from Krassko began making improvements to the bread.

Merchandising experts followed.

Within a year *Our Daily Bread* became global.

Several younger monks decided to form a new bakery.

A few tried to bake *Our Daily Bread* in secret.

Nobody could remember the recipe.

It's not a miracle, it's Placebo®!

Set aside your workaday worries and partake in the amazing panacea known as Placebo®. Placebo is synthetically formulated to speed its healing medicines directly to the source of your maladies. These easy-to-swallow time-release capsules are rapidly absorbed by the body and quickly remedy just about anything (allergies, anxiety, sodomy, and even religious guilt). So try *it today*! If, for any reason, you are not completely satisfied, simply increase the recommended dosage as necessary until you reach the desired effect (numb, giddy, or oblivious).

Placebo is mass-produced under vaguely stringent standards to guarantee maximum potency, and has been clinically tested on helpless animals for over a decade. Human studies, conducted over several months, have not yet detected any clinically significant side effects, outside of a few upset stomachs, sporadic cramping, and severe nausea. In some cases, however, there were isolated incidents involving rather sudden and severe mood swings, road rage, and even acne. But that aside, researchers (ours) still believe that taking Placebo daily can reduce long-term effects of most psychosomatic disorders, with the possible exception of egotism, for some very odd reason.

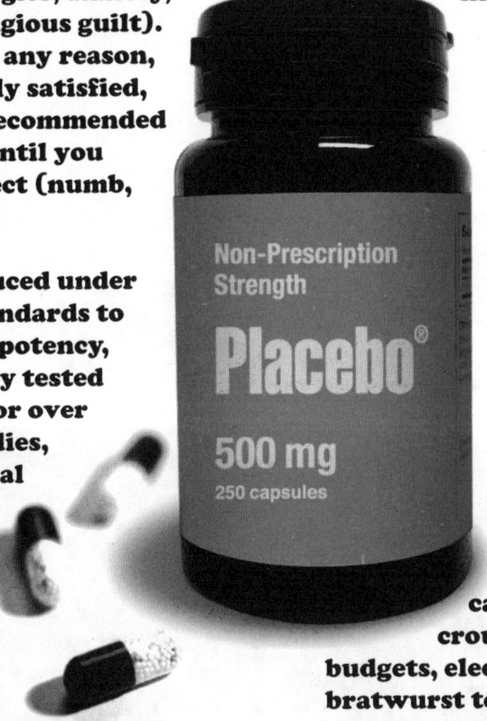

Placebo is recommended by several doctors, and the Lesser Kamtchucka Health Conglomerate (the largest and most celebrated health organization in Lesser Kamtchucka).

Whatever it is that reduces your quality of life is instantly swept under the rug like a minor error in the State of the Union Address. But please be advised, Placebo can become addictive. Once you've begun using it for one ailment, you need to continue usage indefinitely.

Placebo has been proven–under sworn testimony–to have an effect on: tumors, mange, infertility, innuendo, cooties, optimism, sin, distemper, emotional inertia, sunken chest, sallowness, diaper rash, lung butter, hunchbacks, government spending, camel toe, trade deficits, the croup, dorkiness, body odor, budgets, elections, ingrown toenails, bratwurst tongue, self esteem, yellow, scarlet, and tartan fever, poor grammar, incontinence, domestic drug policy, environmentalism, reality television, consumerism, greed, corporate responsiblity, codependency, tolerance, hygiene, and general malaise.

Live each day like it's your last and order your Placebo® cure-all today!

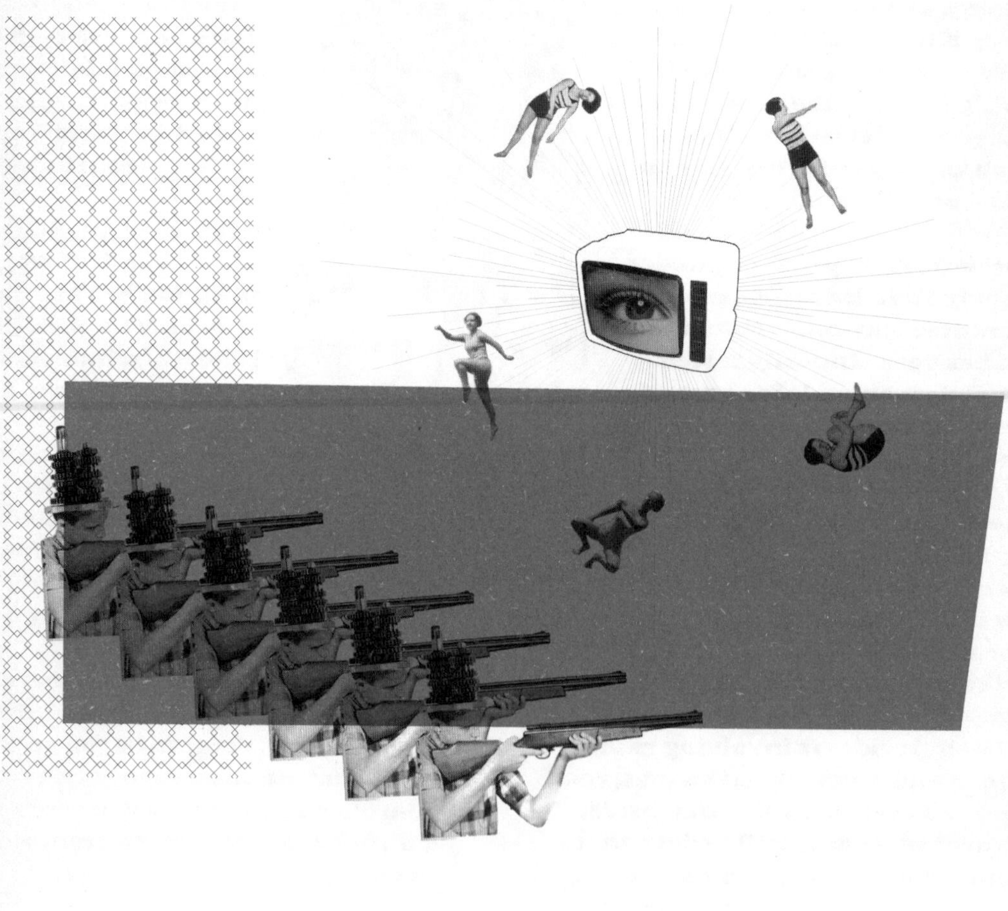

Walk softly & carry a big brand
sherman/03

Think different

1. The Apple Store SoHo, located in the former Prince Street Station Post Office in New York, packs over fifty top-of-the-line computers; hundreds of peripheral devices (cameras, videocameras, scanners, printers, speakers, MP3 players); music, image, and video editing facilities; a 50-seat theater for multimedia presentations and in-store seminars; a "bar" for chatting about Apple products and getting repair service; and more into its airy 18,000 square feet of showroom. The largest Apple Store so far, the Apple Store SoHo is the perfect playground for the digital shopper. Every piece of technology welcomes experimentation: try before you buy.

2. Production supplants consumption in the Apple Store. Prospective buyers are encouraged to try out the computers in-store until they are fully satisfied. This is not the same as trying on a shirt or even test-driving a car. Given the virtual nature of computer work, "testing" and "working/producing" can be identical: I try out Adobe Photoshop by retouching and printing out a photograph for a client. In contrast to purchasing and using a lawnmower, which requires taking the lawnmower home to the grass, one can design a website while in the Apple Store – akin to bringing the lawn to the store. Working preys on shopping.

3. Internet cafes are a thing of the past. Why pay to surf when the Apple Store invites visitors to "try out" the suite of internet programs available in Mac OSX, all over a broadband connection? Purchasing a several-thousand-dollar computer for home or office also becomes a questionable decision in light of the opportunities available at the Apple Store. At no cost, one can check email, scan photographs, download MP3s, burn CDs, shoot digital photographs, design websites, and edit videos – all on the highest-end computers available. Using the Apple Store for personal or professional activities, one becomes a benign parasite. Although not explicitly desired by the management of the Apple Store, such activity is not forbidden. After all, the fuller the store is with people working away happily on Apple computers, writing emails and editing music and burning DVDs of movies, the more evidence that everyone is making the switch.

4. Apple Store SoHo, 103 Prince Street, New York, NY
Mon–Sat: 10am to 8pm, Sun: 11am to 6pm

Note on production: This essay and accompanying floorplan were created exclusively at the Apple Store SoHo using only available computers and programs during January and February 2003.

Apple Store SoHo, ground floor
status 02-25-2003

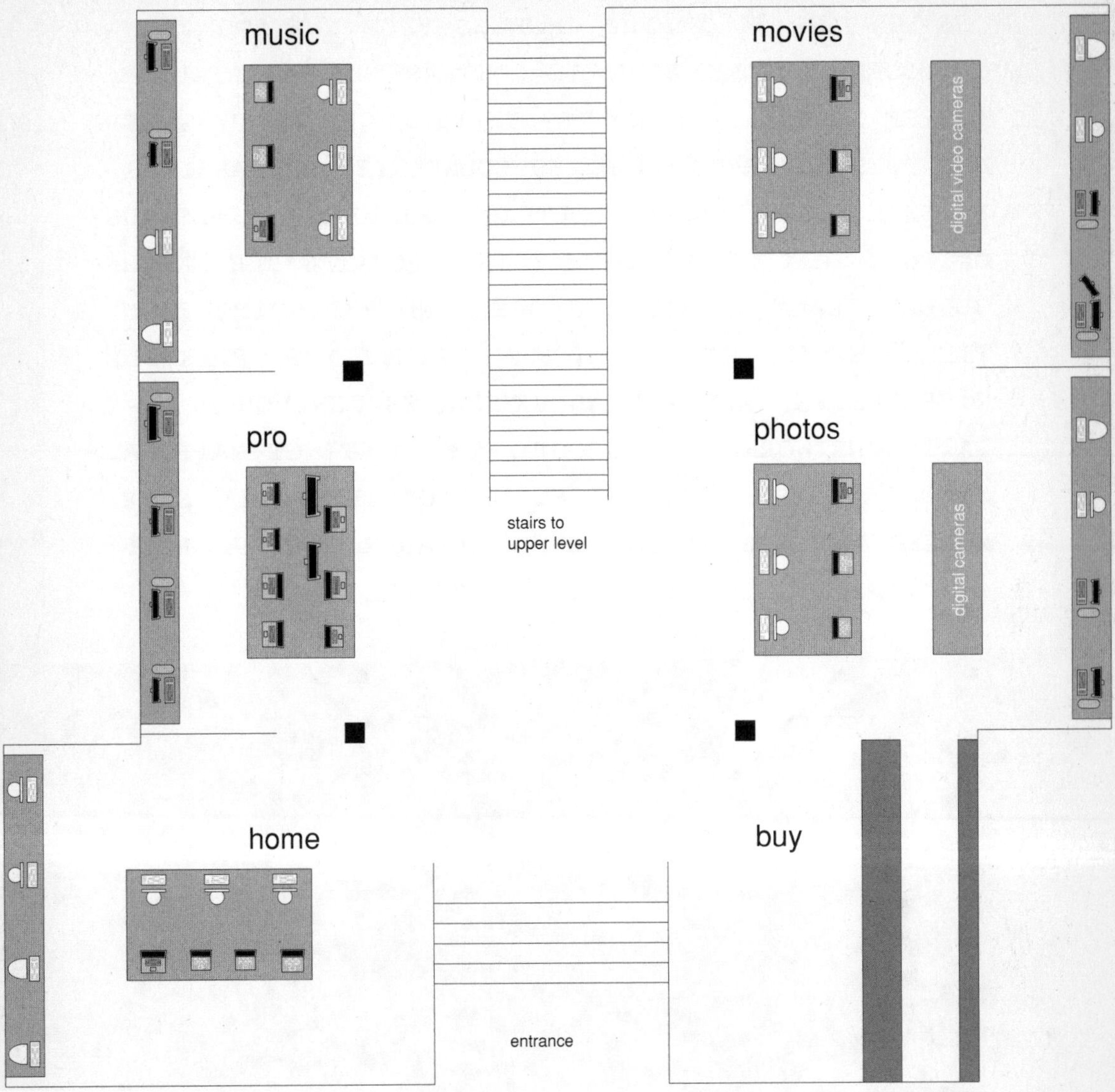

home
The most basic computers are in the home section; nevertheless, they still offer high-speed Internet access and word-processing software among other features.

pro
These high-end computers offer professional page layout, illustration, image manipulation, and motion graphics software.

music
All computers here feature iPods, audio speakers, and the ability to burn CD-ROMs.

photos
Digital cameras and image manipulation software are available at all computers in this section of the store; in addition, the desktop computers are connected to scanners and inkjet printers.

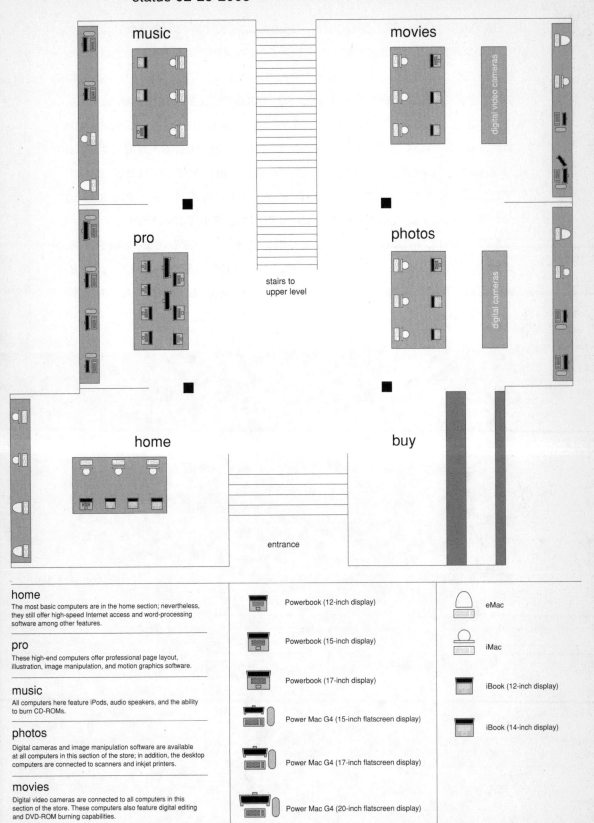

movies
Digital video cameras are connected to all computers in this section of the store. These computers also feature digital editing and DVD-ROM burning capabilities.

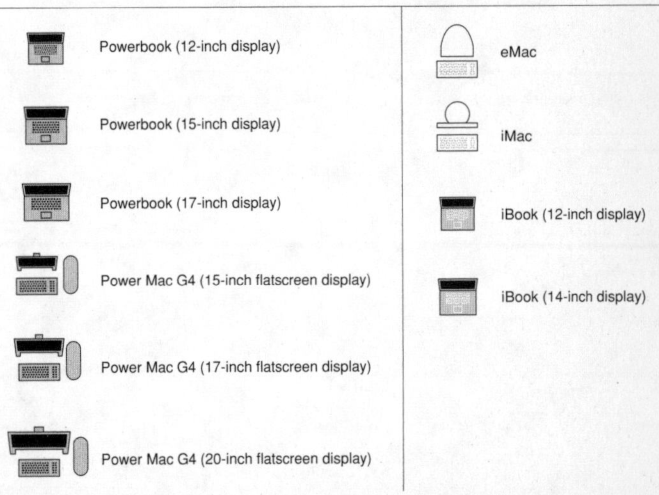

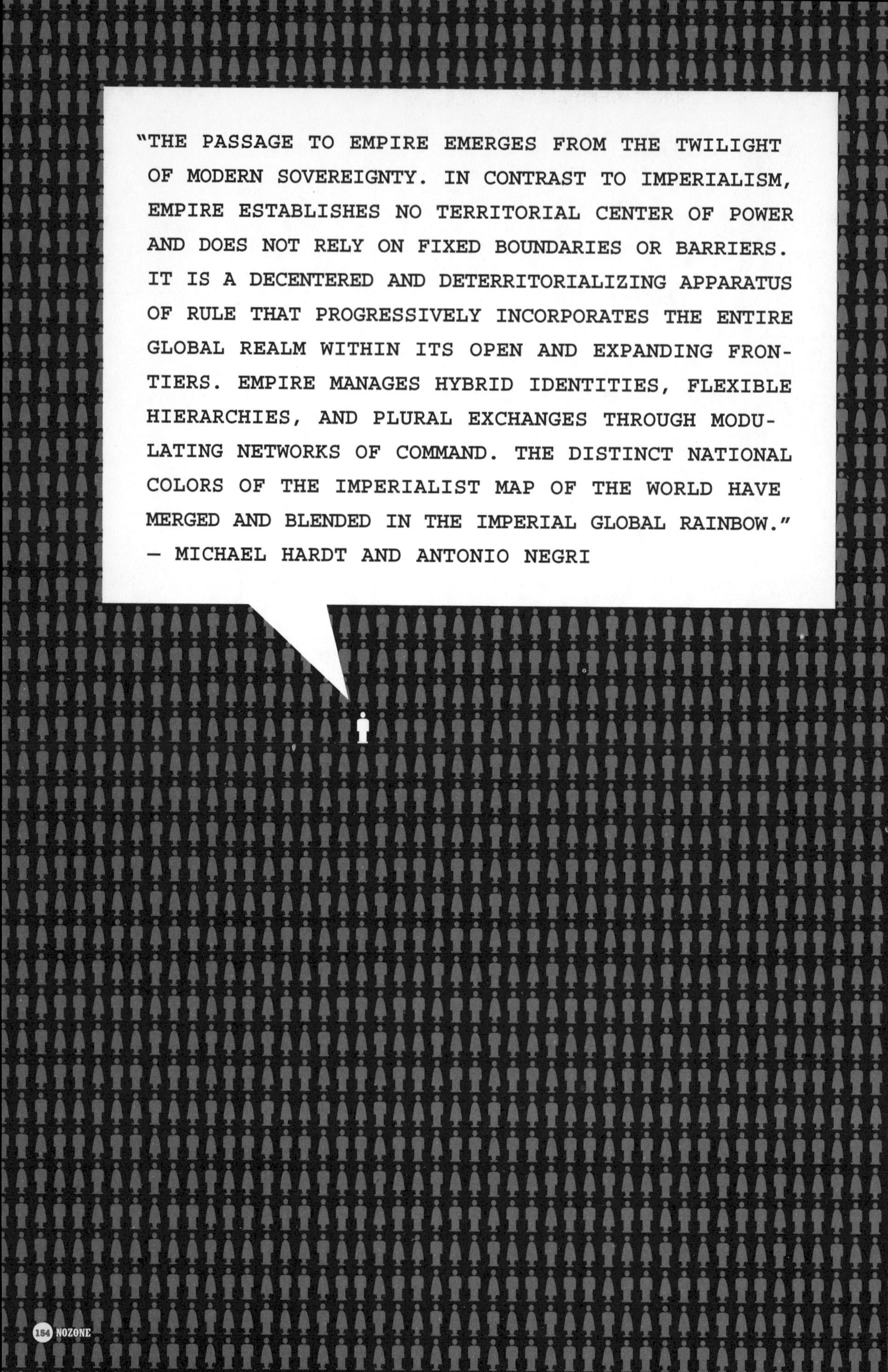
"THE PASSAGE TO EMPIRE EMERGES FROM THE TWILIGHT OF MODERN SOVEREIGNTY. IN CONTRAST TO IMPERIALISM, EMPIRE ESTABLISHES NO TERRITORIAL CENTER OF POWER AND DOES NOT RELY ON FIXED BOUNDARIES OR BARRIERS. IT IS A DECENTERED AND DETERRITORIALIZING APPARATUS OF RULE THAT PROGRESSIVELY INCORPORATES THE ENTIRE GLOBAL REALM WITHIN ITS OPEN AND EXPANDING FRONTIERS. EMPIRE MANAGES HYBRID IDENTITIES, FLEXIBLE HIERARCHIES, AND PLURAL EXCHANGES THROUGH MODULATING NETWORKS OF COMMAND. THE DISTINCT NATIONAL COLORS OF THE IMPERIALIST MAP OF THE WORLD HAVE MERGED AND BLENDED IN THE IMPERIAL GLOBAL RAINBOW."
– MICHAEL HARDT AND ANTONIO NEGRI

THEM
PIRE
© Lobrow

CLIK

15
NEW

15
NE

© Lobrow

"MORE THAN HALF A CENTURY OF ECONOMIC DEPRESSIONS, WORLD WARS, REVOLUTIONS, AND SYSTEMATIC PROGRAMS OF EXTERMINATION HAVE GROUND THE MORAL FOUNDATIONS OF MODERN CIVILIZATION TO RUBBLE AND DUST....THE POWER SYSTEM ITSELF SEEMED NEVER SO FORMIDABLE AS NOW, WITH ONE BRILLIANT TECHNOLOGICAL FEAT FOLLOWING ANOTHER, ITS NEGATIVE LIFE-MUTILATING COUNTERPART HAS NEVER BEEN SO THREATENING."

— LEWIS MUMFORD

NOTES

p.10 Lewis H. Lapham, "The Demonstration Effect," *Harper's* 306, no. 1837 (June 2003): 9.
p.12 Niall Ferguson, *Empire: The Rise and Demise of the British World Order and the Lessons for Global Power* (New York: Basic Books, 2003), 370.
p.22 Dwight D. Eisenhower, "Farewell Radio and Television Address to the American People," 17 January 1961, <http://coursesa.matrix.msu.edu/~hst306/documents/indust.html>
pp.48-49 General Sir Stanley Maude, "The Proclamation of Baghdad," *Harper's* 306, no. 1836 (May 2003): 31.
p.50 Cited in Robert H. Reid, "Rebuilding Iraq, Reasons for War," *Boston Globe*, 31 May 2003, A8.
p.56 Cited in Chalmers Johnson, *Blowback: The Costs and Consequences of American Empire* (New York: Henry Holt, 2001), 9.
p.60 Michael Parenti, *Against Empire* (San Francisco: City Lights Books, 1995), 35.
p.63 William Finnegan "The Economics of Empire," *Harper's* 306, no. 1836 (May 2003): 42.
p.73 Fareed Zakaria, "The Previous Superpower," *New York Times*, Sunday Book Review, 27 July 2003.
p.74 Cited in Bill Gallagher, "High Time for Condi, Colin to Go," *Niagara Falls Reporter*, 23 February 2003, <http://www.niagarafallsreporter.com/gallagher104.html>
p.90 Thomas L. Friedman, "A Theory of Everything" *New York Times*, 1 June 2003, A13.
p.94 Cited in Lapham, "Demonstration Effect," 11.
p.112 Parenti, *Against Empire*, 2.
pp.113-36 Translated from German by Catherine Schelbert.
p.144 Eric Schlosser, *Fast Food Nation: The Dark Side of the All-American Meal* (New York: Harper Collins, 2002), 158-59.
p.154 Michael Hardt and Antonio Negri, *Empire* (Cambridge, Mass.: Harvard University Press, 2000), xii.
p.167 Lewis Mumford, *The Pentagon of Power*, (New York, Harcourt Brace Jovanovich, 1970).

PHOTO SOURCES

p.66 United States: Peter Cunningham; Morocco: Barbara Gauss; Italy: Karin Stauss; Australia: Jesse Gordon; India: J. P. Singh
p.67 Ireland: Elizabeth Amon; Bangladesh: Out of Focus; Spain: Jesse Gordon; Germany: Luise Stauss; Greece: Karin Stauss; Switzerland: Regula Freuler; Russia: Alexandra Stark; Canada: Jaime LeBlanc; Finland: Monika Aichele; Iceland: Hjalti Karlsson; Japan: André Lee; China: Wei Lee; South Korea: André Lee

ACKNOWLEDGEMENTS

Special thanks to the artists, writers, and photographers who made Nozone IX possible. In particular, Monika Aichele, Charles S. Anderson, Steven Appleby, Amy Balkin, Michael Bierut, Richard Boynton, Peter Buchanan-Smith, Art Chantry, Seymour Chwast, Robbie Conal, Gary Clement, Peter Cunningham, Jennifer Daniel, Jeffrey Fisher, John Fulbrooke, Jason Fulford, Amy Gray, Robert Grossman, George Hardie, Brad Holland, Erik Johnson, Prem Krishnamurthy, Peter Kuper, Lewis Lapham, Luba Lukova, Michael Mabry, Josh On, Paul Sahre, Stefan Sagmeister, David Sandlin, Stephen Savage, Whitney Sherman, Edward Sorel, Ward Sutton, Henning Wagenbreth, and Lutz Widmaier.

My profound thanks to Jesse Gordon, who helped conceive the Empire theme on a barstool in Brooklyn and provided invaluable editorial advice, writing, and encouragement.

I am especially grateful to Naomi Mizusaki who helped design this book, and consulted with me throughout its production.

Thanks to André Lee, Ashima Jain, and Jennifer Daniel for their design assistance.

Thanks to Christoph Niemann for his enlightening criticisms, editorial suggestions, and camaraderie.

Thanks to Elizabeth Amon for her invaluable contribution and information gathering.

Thanks to Princeton Architectural Press, especially Nancy Eklund Later, Deb Wood, and my editor, Clare Jacobson.

Thanks to R. O. Blechman for his ruthless honesty and for lending his critical eye, over and over again. Thanks to Moisha and Max Blechman for their encouragement and inspiration.

Thanks to Luise Stauss, for her invisible but crucial support.